Whole Life
Whole Bible

Text copyright © Antony Billington, Margaret Killingray, Helen Parry 2012
The authors assert the moral right to be identified as the authors of this work

Published by
The Bible Reading Fellowship
15 The Chambers, Vineyard
Abingdon OX14 3FE
United Kingdom
Tel: +44 (0)1865 319700
Email: enquiries@brf.org.uk
Website: www.brf.org.uk
BRF is a Registered Charity

ISBN 978 0 85746 017 2
First published 2012
10 9 8 7 6 5 4 3 2 1 0
All rights reserved

Acknowledgments
Unless otherwise stated, scripture quotations are taken from the Holy Bible, New International
Version®, NIV® Copyright © 1973, 1978, 1984, 2011 by Biblica, Inc.™. Used by permission
of Hodder & Stoughton Publishers, a member of the Hachette Livre Group UK. All rights
reserved. 'NIV' is a registered trademark of Biblica, Inc. UK trademark number 1448790.

Extract from 'As water to the thirsty' by Timothy Dudley-Smith (b. 1926) © Timothy Dudley-
Smith in Europe and Africa. © Hope Publishing Company in the United States of America and
the rest of the world. Verse reproduced by permission of Oxford University Press. All rights
reserved.

The paper used in the production of this publication was supplied by mills that source their
raw materials from sustainably managed forests. Soy-based inks were used in its printing and
the laminate film is biodegradable.

A catalogue record for this book is available from the British Library

Printed in Singapore by Craft Print International Ltd

Whole Life
Whole Bible

50 readings
on living in the light of Scripture

Antony Billington

with Margaret Killingray and Helen Parry

*

Contributors

Antony Billington

Antony taught Hermeneutics and Biblical Theology at London School of Theology for 16 years before joining LICC. As Head of Theology, his role is to develop the biblical and theological breadth and depth of the LICC team in their ongoing work with Christians, churches and church leaders. Antony regularly contributes to the life and ministry of the local Baptist church where he is a member. He enjoys spending time with his family and friends, reading, browsing in bookshops, and working his way through DVD box sets of quality TV series.

Margaret Killingray

Margaret has been a part-time lecturer and tutor at LICC since the late 1980s. She has degrees in Sociology and Theology. Before joining LICC, she ran a teachers' centre within London University. She has written a book called *Choices* (BRF, 2001), which explores the influences that shape our thinking as Christians and the difficulty of making moral decisions in the real world. She is also an Anglican Reader and a regular writer for BRF's *Day by Day with God* Bible reading notes. Margaret has been married for almost 50 years to David, a retired professor of history, and has eight grandchildren. She enjoys reading whodunnits, especially those by Donna Leon.

Helen Parry

After training as an English teacher, Helen got married and went straight off to Africa, where she and her husband, Eldryd, taught over a period of 23 years in African universities in Nigeria, Ethiopia and Ghana. On coming back to London, Helen went on a course at LICC, got hooked and has been there ever since. Her role at LICC enables her to indulge two great passions—helping to bring the Bible to life for people and encouraging Christians to develop a global perspective. Helen has four adult children and four grandchildren, who occupy considerable periods of delightful time. She is also involved in teaching and 'global vision' at her church.

*

Preface

The 50 readings in this book began life as a special series of weekly emails sent out by the London Institute for Contemporary Christianity (LICC). From May 2001 onwards, LICC's free email service, Word for the Week, has provided a short reflection on a passage from the Bible, seeking to earth scripture in real-life contexts, and reaching approximately 10,000 subscribers around the world every week. For us, as regular writers of the emails, this weekly commitment provides an ongoing encouragement to keep scripture central to the work and ministry of the Institute as well as the everyday lives of those we aim to serve.

In March 2009, we undertook the challenge of leading subscribers through the main contours of the Bible over the course of a year. The principal idea was to work our way through the biblical story from beginning to end, highlighting key turns in the plot, major characters, important motifs, and the like—but to do so in a way that tried to show how the biblical story nurtures a distinctive way of looking at the world and living in the world. The key driver was to begin to lay down a biblical basis for our emphasis as an Institute on the significance of whole-life discipleship, and to do so not simply by selecting ad hoc Bible passages here and there but by showing that a whole-life emphasis is part and parcel of the biblical narrative, from start to finish. Hence, *Whole Life, Whole Bible*.

Although all three of us have had the opportunity to edit the contributions of each of the other two, our distinctive styles doubtless remain in this finished product. We hope that this will enrich the reading process, providing a combination of theological reflection, pastoral insight and appropriate exhortation, comfort as well as challenge.

We would like to thank members of the LICC team who read the original series as it progressed and told us when we'd 'done good' and where we could 'do better'. Thanks, too, to the many subscribers who emailed us with feedback, often encouraging as well as pushing back on certain points. Thanks also to Mark Coffey for contributing Reading No. 22, bringing to his reflection an authenticity as a teacher at The Manchester Grammar School.

In the process of bringing the readings to publication, we have been helped enormously by the comments of three 'real' readers involved in 'real life'—David Lewis, Claire Robinson and Sue Rugg. No less real, but also wearing his scholarly hat, David Spriggs, Bible and Church Consultant with the Bible Society, pointed out infelicities and made many helpful suggestions which smoothed out some of the rougher edges of the material. Our colleagues Ben Care, Tracy Cotterell and Mark Greene also deserve special mention for their comments and encouragement along the way. Finally, we are grateful to BRF for publishing the readings in this revised format, and especially for the editorial support of Naomi Starkey. All of these people greatly improved the manuscript, though none of them bears any responsibility for the flaws that remain.

The *Whole Life, Whole Bible* readings represent something of LICC's vision and hope for churches and individuals—

that the whole people of God might engage with the whole word of God in a way that touches and transforms the whole of our lives, individually and together, and for the sake of the world in which we are called to live.

Antony Billington
Margaret Killingray
Helen Parry

*

Contents

Covenant

Christ

Church

Consummation

Conclusion

*

Foreword

Not another book on the Bible
(or an invitation to a slow chew)

This one is different.

Honest.

It may not be the only book like it but it is different from lots of other books on the Bible, from most commentaries on the Bible, from a great deal of what's been written and taught about the Bible.

And it's different in a particular and vital way.

It was written for a particular and vital reason, just as John Stott founded LICC for a particular and vital reason. Back in the early 1980s, he saw with searing clarity that somehow the people of God were not able to connect the living word of God to the issues that they faced out in the world. He saw that the church leaders who faithfully and devotedly pastored them and the theological colleges that faithfully and carefully trained church leaders were teaching the Bible, but not necessarily in a way that helped people see that all of their life could be lived for the Lord, or how God's mission could be pursued in work and at school, not just in church buildings and leisure-time activities.

The gospel of Jesus Christ isn't a leisure-time gospel; it's a whole-life gospel, an everyday, every place, every task, mind, heart, spirit, hands and feet and lips gospel.

So this book takes that whole-life gospel perspective really seriously, and seeks to honour the comprehensive scope of the salvation that Jesus invites us to participate in. This book asks, what happens if we read God's word this way? What happens if we read this book through the lens of a whole-life gospel?

Well, I think remarkable things happen: 'ordinary' people see God, see themselves, their situations, their colleagues, their opportunities, their resources, their church communities, in radically different ways. They pray differently, act differently, work differently, study differently, parent differently, play differently, eat differently, speak differently, and reach out to others differently. And that's what the Bible says God's word is meant to do:

All Scripture is God-breathed and is useful for teaching, rebuking, correcting and training in righteousness, so that the servant of God may be thoroughly equipped for every good work. (2 Timothy 3:16–17)

This book focuses on helping us see the whole sweep of scripture through the gospel of Jesus. The chapters are short and you can read them in three minutes or mull over them for much longer.

But though it's made up of bite sized chapters, it's more like a big bag of assorted toffees than a tube of Smarties.

Certainly, you could chomp through the bag quickly, but I suspect you'll find yourself lingering over many of these passages, turning them over in your mind as you might a toffee with your tongue, poking them around your mouth, feeling their contours, letting the flavours develop on your palate... Just read the reflection on the creation of humankind (no. 5) and you'll see what I mean.

As for the authors, well, I confess a conflict of interest. They all work for me. And they are all remarkably gifted but also so self-deprecating and self-effacing that they would read any accolades I might offer and instantly file them under 'fiction'.

I've known Antony Billington for 22 years, and Margaret Killingray and Helen Parry for twelve. They love God's word, they love the God of the word, and their lives are eloquent testimony to their desire to follow and obey him in every area of life. They have all been teaching the Bible all their adult lives. They have done so in a variety of places and a variety of ways to all kinds of people—pastors and students, adults and children, builders and barristers, Brits and Barbadians and Belgians and people from pretty much every nation under the sun—and they continue to teach people how to understand and live God's word week by week.

I commend their work to you. I am very grateful for it. And I hope you will be too.

Enjoy the chew.

Mark Greene
Executive Director, LICC

Start here

And he said to me, 'Son of man, eat what is before you, eat this scroll; then go and speak to the people of Israel.' So I opened my mouth, and he gave me the scroll to eat.

EZEKIEL 3:1–2

It is a crucial lesson for a prophet to learn: his words will not be his own, but God's. He will not have to fabricate his message or concoct it out of thin air. He is assured that what he speaks will be nothing less than God's word. Yet, it has to become his own before he can present it to others. He must absorb it into his own personality. And in that process of 'digestion', the words of God will also be nothing less than Ezekiel's own words. He will sound like he always sounds; his mannerisms will be recognisably those of the son of Buzi; his priestly interest in all things to do with holiness and the temple will be readily apparent (along with his curious penchant for going into more detail about those matters than many of us really care for). Even so, God will embody his own words in the words of a human being, such that Ezekiel's message will be fully God's message.

In Revelation 10:8–10, John undergoes a similar experience. There too we have a dramatic demonstration of a prophet of God internalising the word of God. It's a powerful picture of what we're called to in our own engagement with God's word—not that we will become merely more technically competent in handling scripture, or even that we will just learn more about God and his word, but that his word will become so much more a part of us. It's an encouragement to read the Bible and to be read by the Bible; to read not merely to be informed about God but to be transformed by God. It's a challenge to make sure we do not stand over scripture, seeking to make sense of it, without first making sure we stand under it, allowing it to make sense of us and to shape us from the inside out.[1]

This is a helpful image to keep before us as a directing principle for the ethos of the whole of our lives: as we live for Christ in the contemporary world, we seek to do so in the light of scripture.

That's the conviction throughout the readings in this book—that the Bible itself, God's word, sets the agenda for our lives as followers of Jesus today. And it does so not just in the 'spiritual' matters of the heart or merely with respect to personal values, but in the whole of life—from Monday to Saturday as well as on Sunday, in public and in private, in culture as well as in church, in work as much as in worship. Moreover, this 'whole-life' perspective is not limited to a few biblical passages here and there, but is part of the very warp and woof of scripture, woven through the story as a whole—from creation to new creation, from the garden of Genesis to the city of Revelation.

After this introduction, the book is divided into three parts:

• Setting the scene
• Telling the story
• Taking next steps

This is how the parts play out.

Setting the scene

This section is a mini-guide to what follows. If you're the kind of person who likes to check out maps and guidebooks and travel leaflets before setting out on a journey, start here. This part of the book considers the significance of looking at the big picture of the Bible as a whole, sketches some of the dimensions involved in taking account of the biblical story, and reflects on some of the benefits of doing so.

If you already have some sense of the lie of the land, or if you're the kind of person who likes to stride out into the relative unknown, please feel free to jump to the readings themselves and perhaps come back to this section afterwards.

Telling the story

This, the major part of the book, will take you—via some key passages—through the biblical story from its beginning to its end. We make no claim that this is the only way of telling the story; in fact, several recommended books in the 'Taking next steps' section tell it in different, though complementary, ways. In common with other such Bible overviews, a certain degree of prior knowledge is assumed. This is not a first telling of the Bible story for those who have never encountered it before, but more a retelling for those who are already familiar with its broad contours, who would like the opportunity to get to grips with the story in its entirety and consider how it impacts the whole of life.

Our first concern throughout has been to give the biblical story priority (while acknowledging that the selection of passages already amounts to a kind of interpretive framework), to allow the story to shape our understanding of God, his world, ourselves, and our relationship with him, each other and the created world—broken but now redeemed in Christ, and all the while looking forward to final and full restoration.

The overarching desire to keep the story going has taken precedence over the impulse to find a 'golden nugget' of practical insight in every passage. For instance, telling the story of the Bible arguably has to include the division of the Israelite kingdom after the death of Solomon (Reading 19), even if its relevance to whole-life discipleship is not immediately apparent! But this is precisely the point—that the insights are not always found in the small details so much as in the bigger picture. In fact, in many cases, it's not too difficult to see an implication or to trace a line of thought between the biblical story and our own lives.

Exercises or questions are included with every reading, designed to stimulate further reflection and action, in the hope that the encounter with God's word might affect the heart and hands as well as the head. The exercises allow for different levels of engagement; some suggest following a particular topic through other passages in scripture; some encourage deeper reflection; some suggest points of application or things to try.

We envisage and hope that the readings will be used in different ways in various contexts. Here are just some suggestions.

Reading by yourself

Although the book was not designed to be read straight through in one or two sittings, some might find it helpful to do so in order to get a quick overview. If you're reading by yourself, a better procedure would be to spread the readings over a longer period of time—perhaps one a day for 50 days (or 50 working days), or even one a week for 50 weeks, reading as part of the natural rhythm of your week (first thing on a Monday morning, perhaps, or during your tea and chocolate cake break on a Wednesday afternoon).

Reading with others

Reading the Bible alone is vital for an individual's ongoing relationship with God. Reading with others brings added dimensions. The Bible itself is clear that there is an integral relationship between the word of God and the people of God, in which scripture shapes the way we think and the way we live—together—as part of an ongoing commitment to serve God faithfully, together. Reading with others helps to prevent privatised readings of the Bible and corrects some of the biases we may bring to certain passages or topics. Others see things I don't see; others have insights I don't have; others face challenges I don't face. All of this means that, especially where the group members grow to trust each other, there is great benefit in reading together and sharing together. This being the case, you may find it helpful to go through the readings with others—with a friend or spouse, prayer partners or colleagues at work, or in a church small group—using the questions to prompt discussion.

Reading on location

Whether by ourselves or with others, where we read scripture adds some interesting elements to how we read scripture. An increasing number of people are reading the Bible, alone or with others, in public spaces—coffee shops being an obvious favourite. Once again, there are enormous benefits in doing so, aside from the empowerment that comes from doing something in a group that we might not do if we were alone. Perhaps most significantly, a public context—on the train travelling into work, say—helps to 'normalise' reading the Bible, making it natural to seek connections with the day ahead, encouraging us to think how the Bible relates not just to us in our everyday contexts, but to the people around us—the harassed parent, the young accountant, the lonely pensioner.

Taking next steps

Many of the exercises attached to each reading suggest some specific next steps in reflection and response. In addition, this final section recommends other resources on scripture and discipleship, which will take further the journey embarked on here.

Setting the scene

The 'tipping point' might come about through a probing conversation at work, a family incident or a forced change of circumstances, or via consistently faithful teaching in church, a good book or a casual conversation with a fellow Christian. However the realisation dawns, at some point today's disciples of Christ discover what the first disciples discovered, that being a follower of Jesus involves much more than changing a few features of our lifestyle here and there. It requires a complete reordering of the whole of our existence in loving service to Christ himself, whose call embraces every area of our lives. How we should understand the biblical basis of this comprehensive call and its implications for everyday life is the burden of this book. As the title suggests and as the readings seek to show, such whole-life discipleship is best funded by the whole of God's word: whole-life disciples are to be whole-Bible disciples, those who are shaped by the big picture of scripture.

Whole Bible: reading the story of life

As it happens, 'story' has become a significant category in contemporary discussion, with many suggesting that one of the characteristics that marks human beings out as distinctive is that we are story-making and story-telling animals. Every day of our lives, we do things or things happen to us or other people's lives intersect with ours, and—often without even thinking about it—we link these 'events' and 'characters' together in a sequence that makes sense of them and gives meaning to them, a sequence that, if we were asked to do so, we could relay to others. We all have and tell and are submerged in various interconnecting 'stories', all of which shape our lives in different ways.

For Christians, however, the most crucial story for determining our identity, for shaping the way we think and live, is the biblical story. Moreover, story is the primary means through which God has chosen to reveal himself in scripture. From Genesis to Revelation, from the garden of Eden to the city of the new Jerusalem, the whole Bible can be seen as an epic narrative: a story that begins with God as Creator, focuses on Israel as the people who will bring God's blessing to the nations, and (the New Testament declares) has come to its promised fulfilment in the redemption brought about through Christ, the one in whom God's purposes for the universe will be consummated.

In fact, the broad contours, or main acts, of the biblical story line can be highlighted in six words:[2]

- Creation
- Corruption
- Covenant
- Christ
- Church
- Consummation

Christians look to the biblical account of *creation* for their understanding of what it means to be human, created in the image of God. The opening chapters of Genesis describe the place of humans in relationship to the world and to each other, as well as our capacity to relate with God. They affirm that the material world was created good, that man and woman were created good, that male–female complementarity is good, that procreation is good. Alas, the story goes on to show us that things don't stay good.

Corruption creeps in. We see how sin has tragic effects on our relationship with the world, with each other and with God. The Bible pictures the harsh reality of human existence under the rule of sin: men and women rebel against God and are unfaithful to each other; they become alienated from others, relating through suspicion, envy, greed, pride and anger.

Thankfully, the biblical story goes on to show how God makes a *covenant* with a chosen people. It tells of God's promises to Abraham, and the beginning of the nation with the patriarchs. The people go to Egypt during Joseph's time and then out of Egypt with Moses at the exodus. There is the confrontation with God at Sinai, the giving of the law, the sacrificial system, the tabernacle and the establishment of the priesthood. Then, what follows is the taking over of Canaan, the promised land, under Joshua, and eventually the rise of the monarchy, with David settling the ark of the covenant in Jerusalem, followed by the building of the temple. After Solomon, however, comes the division of the kingdom into north and south, with God's judgment coming upon both kingdoms, the south eventually going off into captivity in the sixth century BC, with the subsequent restoration back to the land under Ezra and Nehemiah. Among all these events arise a number of ways of looking forward to the coming of a 'redeemer' figure—an anointed one, a prophet like Moses, a priest in the order of Melchizedek, a king, a son of man—all meshed into the story.

Then the story tells of God becoming flesh and living among us in *Christ*. God himself is embodied as a human being—not as an end in itself, but because the only way humanity can be rescued from sin and its consequences is through the restoration achieved by Jesus' death on the cross on our behalf, in order to bring about renewed relationship with God, with each other and, ultimately, with the rest of creation.

The story doesn't end there, for Christians meanwhile belong to the *church* of Christ, a people in whom God's Spirit lives, which shapes our character and mission in distinctive ways. Under the new covenant, the people of God are no longer a nation with geographical boundaries; the people of God are now an international community, themselves the temple of God's presence, with God's law written on their hearts. And we look forward to the *consummation* of all things—Jesus' return, new resurrected bodies and the remaking of the universe. Until then, we remain on the way to becoming fully restored, our identity finally complete at the end of the story as we join with all nations walking in the light of the Lamb.

Even to relate the story in this way (and to acknowledge that others may tell aspects of the story differently) is to show that the Bible doesn't offer a bare chronicle of historical facts, but tells a narrative that carries theological significance, in which we see God at work—creating, judging, promising salvation, lovingly and faithfully working out his plan of restoration. It should come as no surprise, then, that this all-encompassing plan of salvation carries implications for the lives of those called to follow Christ.

Whole life: following the Lord of life

Knowing the ingredients of the story is one thing; under-standing the import of the story is something else. We limit ourselves here to highlighting three implications of the big story of scripture for our lives as disciples of Christ.

1. For building our understanding

Survey after survey in recent years—carried out with people in churches, leaders and non-leaders, as well as non-church people—has confirmed that there is an increasing lack of biblical literacy in the church, not only in society more generally. The surveys reveal that the vast majority of people in churches feel positive about the Bible and consider it to be revelation from God, but fewer and fewer, it seems (even church leaders), are reading it for themselves. And when we do manage to read it, the surveys suggest, we're not always sure what to do with it.

Some might go so far as to say that there is a crisis of con-fidence in the Bible. This is largely because of the questions it raises. One of the understandable temptations, perhaps, is to want quick answers to all the difficult issues—about creation and evolution, about the strange laws, about the harsh violence, about the bizarre visions, about men and women, about same-sex relationships, and so on. But those questions are better addressed, and more securely answered, when we have a larger framework in place.

Looking at the big story of the Bible offers a crucial means of helping to address the issue of growing biblical illiteracy, because it provides a way not just of getting to know the 'bits and pieces' of the content of the Bible (individual stories or passages), but of understanding how those bits and pieces relate to each other in the grand story. As we would hope and expect, increased knowledge of the parts over time strengthens understanding of the whole, as well as building confidence in knowing how to handle the seemingly more tricky parts of the Bible. A strengthening in our understanding of scripture's big picture also develops our trust in God himself as we see him faithfully working out his plan of salvation through history.

2. For forming our worldview

Christian thinkers have sometimes compared the Bible to a pair of spectacles. We look through scripture as through a set of lenses to see God, the world around us and ourselves more clearly. This being the case, it is the big story of the Bible that best informs and forms our worldview. God's word gets 'inside' us, as it did for Ezekiel when he was called to eat the scroll handed to him by the Lord (Ezekiel 2:8—3:3), and transforms us—transforms the way we think about the world, so that we begin to see things as God sees them. In crafting a Christian worldview, then, we do so on the basis of the biblical story and its major plot points: God's original creation, the tragedy of sin, and God's plan of redemption, set in motion through Israel, fulfilled in Christ, lived out through the church and awaiting final consummation.

This is one of the central points made by Craig Bartholomew and Michael Goheen in their book, *The Drama of Scripture*. In a culture where many stories shape us and compete to describe the nature of reality, it's the biblical story that should be central to the formation of a Christian worldview. They argue that we mustn't try to fit the Bible into a convenient space in our world, but must fit our world into the Bible, to find our place in the story of the Bible, to immerse ourselves in it, so that we begin to think and live out of its perspective. Then the whole biblical story will shape our worldview and mould the way we view God, the world and ourselves.[3]

3. For shaping our discipleship

It's not too much of a stretch to move from considering the Bible as a narrative to considering it as a drama, which also makes it possible for us to think in terms of performance— how we live out the story. Hence, we are partakers rather than spectators: every one of us, in our own individual way, has a role in the continuing drama of God's unfolding purposes.

What we need to do, according to this 'drama' analogy, is to immerse ourselves in the biblical script, to live imaginatively in its account of the world, to gain a deep appreciation of the mind of the author and the movement of the story. In doing so, over time, we grow in our understanding of what it means to be created beings, our realisation that the world is not what it should be, our joyful apprehension that Christ became flesh, lived among us, suffered and died, and our delight in the goal of God's work for the whole of creation. In short, we seek to find our place in God's story, so that it becomes *our* story. We live in such a way that we seek to embody God's original intent for creation as well as the hope of consummation, guided by the way God has shaped his people in communities in Israel and the church. And the story shapes us in the process: it shapes how we think and how we live, our giving, our hospitality, our use of time, our sexual activity, our business deals, our political views, the way we bring up our kids, the way we relate to each other, and the way we see the world and people in the world.

It fashions us in these areas because it's a story that begins with the creation of all things and ends with the renewal of all things. It's a story that is creation-affirming rather than world-denying, in which God continues to maintain the world he created. It's a story in which men and women were created in his image to enjoy communion with him and each other, and to exercise loving and responsible stewardship over every field of human endeavour in his good creation. It's a story which reminds us that while sin cuts us off from relationship with God and the effects of sin spoil every aspect of life, yet God, out of his love and free grace, brings about complete restoration through the cross of Christ. It's a story which provides a vision of God's kingdom that is as broad as life itself, which encourages us to grasp the amazing reach and comprehensive scope of the gospel and Christ's Lordship, as we are called to embody his rule in our everyday lives as homemakers, teachers, artists, businesspeople, athletes, politicians, lawyers, journalists, labourers and nurses.

The Lord of life calls us to live our lives in the light of his word.

Telling the story

*

Introduction

1: The Lordship of Christ

The Son is the image of the invisible God, the firstborn over all creation. For in him all things were created: things in heaven and on earth, visible and invisible, whether thrones or powers or rulers or authorities; all things have been created through him and for him... God was pleased to have all his fullness dwell in him, and through him to reconcile to himself all things, whether things on earth or things in heaven, by making peace through his blood, shed on the cross.

COLOSSIANS 1:15–16, 19–20

Jesus... Well, where else could we start exploring the main contours of the biblical story? With creation, perhaps? Yes, and we will get to it soon—though we shall find Jesus there before us. Or, on the basis that we best understand the beginning from the perspective of the end, could we start with the consummation of all things? Again, yes, and that will be in our sights—though we shall find Christ there ahead of us.

Paul wrote letters, not narratives, but it is the biblical story that funds his pastoral engagement with churches, and that story sometimes bubbles to the surface, as it does here in Colossians 1:15–20 (and Philippians 2:5–11), where we are taken from creation to consummation through the cross in six verses. And at the heart of it all is Jesus.

So, we begin with the one who embraces both beginning and end, who stands at the heart of God's plan for the ages, himself the image of the invisible God, the Lord of creation and redemption—for the sake of his church. Since all things were made through him and all things will be finalised in him, there is nothing left that does not come under his Lordship. The creator, sustainer and reconciler of all is none other than Jesus, the Lord of all.

Along with the confession of Jesus as Lord goes the assurance that there is no part of ordinary, everyday reality that falls outside the orbit of his loving oversight. As Paul makes clear in the rest of Colossians, Christ's Lordship has implications for every area of life—to the extent that what funds our discipleship, our marriages, our working days and our engagement with the world in which we live is not just the truth about Jesus as creator and redeemer of all things, but our relationship with him as Lord and with each other as his people.

Jesus is Lord—begin here.

For further reflection and action

1. How does Colossians 1:15–20 broaden our horizons on life, and what difference might that make to how we go about our next task, our next conversation, our next meeting, our next purchase?

2. Read and reflect on Philippians 2:5–11, noting from the immediate context (2:1–4 and 12–18) how those who are 'in Christ' are shaped by the story of Christ.

3. In the first-century Roman imperial context, where Caesar is in charge, there are political implications in confessing Jesus as Lord. What are the imperial rulers—the 'Caesars'—of today? How do they exercise their 'lordship', and how does Christ's rule subvert theirs?

2: I'll tell you a story

My people, hear my teaching;
listen to the words of my mouth.
I will open my mouth with a parable;
I will utter hidden things, things from of old—
things we have heard and known,
things our ancestors have told us.
We will not hide them from their descendants;
we will tell the next generation
the praiseworthy deeds of the LORD,
his power, and the wonders he has done.
PSALM 78:1–4

Human beings tell stories, stories that weave individuals and their families into wider communities of place and time. They sing the story of the ancestors who built their village; they learn of the Romans who came and named their towns; they ferret around in the archives to discover their Russian great-grandparents; they say, 'I'm Scottish', 'My grandmother was a slave', 'My father was in the D-Day landings'. And so, through story, they tie themselves in to place and time.

The Bible, the story of humankind's relationship with God, also tells stories. In fact, one story unfolds from beginning to end, with many contributing stories of individuals and nations, which reflect, repeat and enlarge the grand narrative. This narrative (as we saw in our first reading) holds Jesus Christ at the heart of it—Alpha and Omega, creator, redeemer and final judge.

So, the psalmist says, listen to the story; tell it to your children—how God brought you out of slavery under the sign of the lamb's blood and led you on a journey to nationhood. That story is told over and over again in the Old Testament, and it illuminates a new and greater story of the Lamb of God who takes away the sin of the world. In that process, it invests with new profundity other stories: the day of Atonement, Isaiah's suffering servant, the lamb silent before its shearers.

When the pivotal moment of the whole history of God's dealings with humanity took place, and a newborn baby was laid in a manger, Matthew tells us that this baby was part of the human story. His family line descended from the great heroes of God's people, Abraham and David, but also from the smaller stories of faithfulness and redemption, such as Ruth the Moabite and Bathsheba the Hittite (see Matthew 1:1–17).

We too have the privilege of hearing the story and recognising our own place in it. 'Although the whole earth is mine, you will be for me a kingdom of priests and a holy nation,' the Lord told the Israelites at Sinai (Exodus 19:5–6); and, through Peter (1 Peter 2:9), he tells us—the scattered people of God—that *we* are now that holy nation and priestly kingdom, looking ahead to the time when the final curtain comes down on the old world and we reign with him in a renewed earth.

For further reflection and action

1. Some of the psalms tell the story of God's dealings with his people—for example, Psalms 68, 78, 105, 106 and 136. Read and reflect on a few of these. As Christians, we own this as our family story, too: it is as much about us as about Israel. What hints do these psalms provide as to how the story shapes our everyday lives as disciples of Christ?

2. In addition to some of the psalms, other places in scripture summarise the story to a certain point in time: see Deuteronomy 1—4; 26:5–10; Joshua 23—24; Judges 1—2; 1 Samuel 12; 2 Kings 17; Nehemiah 9; Ezekiel 16; 20; 23; Daniel 9; Acts 7:2–52; 13:16–41. Again, read a few of these passages and consider what features keep recurring in the telling of the story (this might provide clues as to what is seen as significant), and think about why the story is being told (that is, what does the teller of the story want to achieve by telling the story?).

3. 'Christians are not utopians. Although we know the transforming power of the gospel and the wholesome effects of Christian salt and light, we also know that evil is ingrained in human nature and human society. We harbour no illusions. Only Christ at his second coming will eradicate evil and enthrone righteousness for ever.'[4] How would you support this statement on the basis of the story the Bible tells?

*

Creation

3: And God…

In the beginning God created the heavens and the earth… This is the account of the heavens and the earth when they were created, when the LORD God made the earth and the heavens.
GENESIS 1:1; 2:4

Our first steps in Genesis begin neither with creation nor with ourselves, but with God—and the reminder that we do not properly understand the world (or our place in it) without acknowledging the God who created it, holds it together and rules over it.

Genesis 1 was designed to work this way. The people of God knew that the real God—the only God—made the world not through violence and bloodshed (a regular feature of tales about origins told in cultures surrounding Israel) but by his word, through his wisdom, and out of love. The account thus shapes the way God's people think and live, at the same time as engaging with alternative takes on reality, in such a way as to say, '*This* is the true God; *this* is what the true God is like; *this* is the one who alone is worthy of worship.'

Genesis 1 does this not by discussing creation in the abstract but by focusing on God as creator, and not primarily through nouns or adjectives but through verbs, highlighting what God does: he creates, he speaks, he sees, he names, he separates, he rules, he delights, he blesses, he rests. This God who speaks and acts will take centre stage in the plot that unfolds, showing that, far from removing himself from creation, he is personal and relational, intentionally providing an arena in which men and women can live under his rule and blessing.

It's no surprise, then, that while Genesis 1:1 can use the non-specific word for 'god' or 'gods', Genesis 2:4 makes it clear that he is 'the LORD God', using the name by which he later reveals himself to Moses as the one who will establish a covenant with his people, setting up a link between creation and covenant that will be played out in the rest of scripture.

Genesis 1 isn't designed to satisfy our curiosity about issues raised by science. A different and more significant question is at stake, namely: which God do we trust to have the whole world in his hands? Standing at the heart of the Christian worldview is not a god of our own making, but the Lord God himself—creator God and covenant God.

For further reflection and action

1. Take some moments to read through Genesis 1:1—2:4, pausing after the account of each day to reflect on—and then to praise—God as creator, sustainer and ruler of all.

2. In Proverbs 8:22–31, God's wisdom is personified as a craftsperson through whom God makes the world—designing, measuring and setting boundaries in place—showing that wisdom is the standard by which God works as he crafts the world. This being the case, where do we see evidence of God's wise ordering of the world? What difference should this make to the way we seek to live in God's world?

3. What do you bring to your reading of Genesis 1 in terms of background education, church tradition, scientific knowledge and convictions about God? How might these various factors both help and hinder your understanding of the passage?

4: It was good

God saw all that he had made, and it was very good.
GENESIS 1:31

'Good.'

There can be no mistaking how God evaluates his creation. The affirmation comes six times in Genesis 1, to make sure we don't miss it. The repetition makes it clear that each part is good, climaxing at the seventh time with the statement that the sum of the parts is 'very good'. God doesn't just create the world; he creates the world *good*—very good.

The fact that the word is applied to stars and seas and trees and turtles suggests that something more than moral goodness is in mind. Think 'good' in the sense that Genesis 1 itself implies: a well-ordered, beneficial, fitting, beautiful, teeming-with-life, everything-in-its-place goodness. From the intricate parts to the immense parts, all of it is good.

Nor is the goodness of creation to be limited to 'nature'. Human society and culture are also embraced, with the goodness of work and marriage affirmed as spheres in which we may serve God—the architect at her desk, the baker in his kitchen, the mother in her home, the teacher in his class, the husband and wife in their bed. All of it good.

For Christians, it is a reminder on the first page of the

Bible that our faith is world-affirming, that we may delight in the goodness of God's created order. It should come as no surprise when God wants to show up in areas of our lives from which he has sometimes been excluded—our careers, our friendships, our studies—since the world has been designed with our well-being in mind, as a place of blessing for us.

Alas, things don't stay good. But the evil that comes later is not an inevitable or necessary part of the fabric of the world or of human beings, and the Bible anticipates a time when evil will be removed. Meanwhile, God's good creation provides a strong clue that 'being saved' by God is not about being released from an evil body for a non-material existence. We may expect that the salvation Christ brings is not a rescue from the world but a salvation for which the world was made in the first place—a new creation, no less (2 Corinthians 5:17).

Much more than a claim about the process by which life came into being, a biblical perspective on creation involves a response of praise to the God on whom the whole of life depends, and who is the source of everything that is good.

For further reflection and action

1. What do today's different 'voices' say about the physical and cultural and social world in which we live? (Think politicians, media pundits, lobby groups, and so on.) How far do these voices square with Genesis 1?
2. Reflect on the actual difference the 'goodness' of creation will make to specific areas of your life today and this week—your work, rest, family, money or time. How do we live distinctly as servants of God in his good creation?

3. It has been regularly noted that on days 1–3 God forms the world (Genesis 1:3–13), and on days 4–6 he fills the world (Genesis 1:14–27). What he separates on days 1–3, he stocks on days 4–6, first making the 'realms' and then assigning their 'rulers'. What might this suggest about the literary qualities of the creation account? And what might this careful structuring of the account teach us about the nature of God's work in creation, and creation itself?

5: The first great commission

Then God said, 'Let us make mankind in our image, in our likeness, so that they may rule over the fish in the sea and the birds in the sky, over the livestock and all the wild animals, and over all the creatures that move along the ground.'

So God created mankind in his own image,
in the image of God he created them;
male and female he created them.

God blessed them and said to them, 'Be fruitful and increase in number; fill the earth and subdue it. Rule over the fish in the sea and the birds in the sky and over every living creature that moves on the ground.'

GENESIS 1:26–28

What is to be the role of human beings in the story about to unfold?

It's the sixth day, and the author of Genesis 1 makes it clear—through devoting more space to it, through repetition, through the divine 'let us' which first plans and then executes the plan—that something even more significant is about to happen. Now the creator forms a creature unlike any of the others, who bears his image.

We give thanks that we have been created with the capacity for emotion, the ability to think and communicate—like God himself—although it's not apparent that his 'image' should be identified with these abilities. It *is* clear that man and woman together constitute the image of God, and that humans are made for relationship with each other as well as with God. Even so, sexual differentiation extends to dolphins, chickens and elephants as well—making it an integral part of God's design for the world but not necessarily the most significant point about being made in his image.

More notable is the connection of the image with the vocation of men and women to rule creation, as representatives of God on earth, charged with the task of 'dominion' over other creatures. Cultures surrounding Israel told creation stories in which people were made as slaves of the gods, with the language of 'image' applied only to kings. In Genesis, however, all human beings are created in the image of God, giving men and women a status and responsibility not found in other worldviews.

Genesis 1 continues to shape our views of humanity—and our lifestyles, too—since the tasks of 'filling', 'subduing' and 'ruling' have not been taken away. In the first place, of course, these words refer to the building of families, the growing of crops and breeding of animals, the tending of the garden to which Adam is called. Creation requires cultivation.

Such cultivation, though, provides the basis of the organisation of society and includes, by extension, the development of culture and civilisation—building houses, designing clothes, writing poetry, playing chess. These are the 'mundane' ways in which we, this very day, exercise our creation mandate, as we represent God's rule over every type of cultural activity, in relationship with others and in a way that reflects God's own nurturing, creative hand.

For further reflection and action

1. Try to spend some time reflecting on the fact that the first purpose of humanity is not 'spiritual' (in terms of the way that word is commonly understood), but the somewhat ordinary category of exercising stewardship over our earthly environment as God's representatives. This being the case, what is it that occupies the bulk of your waking hours? Work, education, home, childcare? How is the image of God demonstrated in these areas of life?

2. Read and reflect on Psalm 8 and its links to Genesis 1. In what ways does its portrayal of human beings as 'crowned with glory and honour' (v. 5) shape our perceptions of ourselves and others?

3. If our fellow human beings, Christian and non-Christian alike, share the mandate to 'cultivate' the earth, what are the implications for the way we treat their work, art, products and so on? Are there any areas of cultural 'cultivation' that might be considered suspect? Advertising, cosmetics, fashion, interior design, contemporary art, weapons manufacturing?

*

Corruption

6: How *could* they?

When the woman saw that the fruit of the tree was good for food and pleasing to the eye, and also desirable for gaining wisdom, she took some and ate it. She also gave some to her husband, who was with her, and he ate it.

GENESIS 3:6

However we interpret the first three chapters of Genesis, they are fundamental to an understanding of our faith, the shaping of our worldview, and our lives as disciples of Christ.

The core sin of Adam and Eve was their disobedience to God's explicit command, 'You must not eat from the tree...' (Genesis 2:17). It was a transgression (the crossing of a forbidden frontier) and thus, inevitably, a revolt against God. The prohibition represented a limitation on the behaviour of the man and the woman, who were otherwise given extraordinary freedom to explore and harness God's creation; and it was an assertion, in the exercise of that freedom, of the ultimate authority of God.

There's a widespread belief outside the church that Christianity is a highly negative religion—with our freedom being curtailed at every turn by a 'thou shalt not'. But, perhaps surprisingly, negative commands give more freedom than positive ones. Thus, rather than giving Adam and Eve handbooks on rearing cattle or pruning trees or making love ('Now this is exactly what to do'), God gave them the liberty to find out for themselves how to do things, and the joy of making their own discoveries.

This included, of course, the liberty to make mistakes. The transgression, however, was more than a mistake: they could hardly have turned to the Lord and said, 'Oh, so sorry, we forgot.' They thought they knew better than God and made a conscious choice to go against his clear will.

It seems almost incredible that Adam and Eve, living among the lavish gifts of the creation (yet to be explored), their wills not yet corrupted by sin, should have succumbed to the seductions of one of the very creatures over whom they had been given dominion. But succumb they did—and that 'original sin', committed by the parents of the human race, was passed on, like a hereditary disease, throughout that race. Humanity, as Psalm 51 reminds us, has borne its stain ever since: 'sinful from the time my mother conceived me' (Psalm 51:5).

And yet, as crucial as this chapter is for the unfolding of the plot that follows, the great story of the Bible doesn't begin or end here. It begins with an unspoiled creation and ends, by way of the resurrection, with a restored new creation—with the nations walking in the light of God's glory (Revelation 21:24).

For further reflection and action

1. The serpent tempted Adam and Eve through their God-given faculties of taste, sight and aspiration. In what areas of life, and by what means, are you most vulnerable to temptation?

2. Read Romans 5:12–21, noting how the biblical story of sin and salvation underlines Paul's contrast between Adam and Christ.

3. How far does it matter to you whether there was a real Adam and Eve, actual trees with fruit, and a talking snake, and how far are you happy to accept them as 'word pictures' to describe deeper realities of human experience of temptation, failure and a sense of shame and guilt? Why do you hold the opinion you do?

7: The fruit of fruit-eating

The man and his wife heard the sound of the LORD God as he was walking in the garden in the cool of the day, and they hid from the LORD God among the trees of the garden.

GENESIS 3:8

John Milton, in the opening lines of his magnificent epic poem *Paradise Lost*, announces his intention to proclaim:

… man's first disobedience, and the fruit
Of that forbidden tree, whose mortal taste
Brought death into the world, and all our woe.[5]

Paradise lost, indeed. Inexorably, the consequences of Adam and Eve's sin unfold. First they feel the new sensations of shame and fear; next come self-justification and mutual recrimination—shame and fear towards God, and recrimination towards each other. Thus, in a few masterful verses, the writer of Genesis records the breakdown of these two key relationships.

The banishment of Adam and Eve from the garden now seems inevitable. Gone is the intimacy with which they could relate to the creator. Worse still, perhaps, the prospect of their eating from the tree of life and thus living for ever is now unthinkable. The expulsion symbolises the gulf that, from that moment onwards, stood between humanity and God—God who is the source of life. As Paul says, 'the wages of sin is death' (Romans 6:23).

But the tragedy doesn't stop with the man and the woman. The whole created order is in some way implicated—in the pain of childbirth, male domination, inhospitable land and toilsome work, which still dominate human experience here on earth. All of these—and many other ways in which the world has fallen from its original 'goodness'—are presented as the result of the humans' initial rebellion. 'All our woe,' wrote Milton, blind, twice widowed and politically disillusioned.

Thus, as the Old Testament moves on, we see recurring cycles of disobedience and idolatry, hatred, pride and corruption. In the wider world, to this very day, human history has been beset by greed, ambition, cruelty, injustice, oppression, the corruption of creativity and the destruction of the environment.

Easy as it is to bewail the state of the world, we must all acknowledge that these destructive tendencies run through every human heart. Our first legacy is the image of God. Parasitic upon it—but not obliterating it—is the legacy of sin. But, as Milton goes on to remind us, the victory of sin could continue only:

... till one greater man
Restore us, and regain the blissful seat.

For further reflection and action

1. 'Inhospitable land and toilsome work.' How far do we feel that this describes our own daily experience? What about the experience of family members, friends and colleagues?

2. How would you evaluate the view that sees Genesis 3 as an unfortunate but minor 'blip' in the biblical story?

3. Which aspect of the opening chapters of the Bible has had the greatest influence on the way you view life—creation or corruption?

8: The way we are

Lamech married two women, one named Adah and the other Zillah. Adah gave birth to Jabal; he was the father of those who live in tents and raise livestock. His brother's name was Jubal; he was the father of all who play stringed instruments and pipes. Zillah also had a son, Tubal-Cain, who forged all kinds of tools out of bronze and iron. Tubal-Cain's sister was Naamah. Lamech said to his wives,

'Adah and Zillah, listen to me;
wives of Lamech, hear my words.
I have killed a man for wounding me,
a young man for injuring me.
If Cain is avenged seven times,
then Lamech seventy-seven times.'

GENESIS 4:19–24

Lamech typifies the contradiction within human existence. He enjoys God's blessing of marriage... but (whether due to the desire for descendants or the passion for prestige) humanity has departed from God's original 'one flesh' design (see Genesis 2:24). And he uses his God-given creativity to compose lines of poetry... which boast of excessive revenge and murder. Yet he fathers three sons, one of whom grazes cattle, one of whom makes music, and one of whom works with metal. Even this family advances agriculture, arts and technology in fulfilment of the creation mandate.

The tension is no surprise to those who take seriously the goodness of God's original design but also recognise that we no longer live in Eden. We still bear God's image, though it is damaged; and the tasks of subduing and ruling remain, though they are distorted. All of this means that we can be neither naively optimistic nor overly pessimistic about ourselves, other people, or the things we turn our hands to—like agriculture and arts and technology. Through these activities we simultaneously demonstrate that we are made in the image of God and act out our rebellion against him, our alienation from each other and our exploitation of the created world.

In such a context—'east of Eden' (Genesis 4:16)—sin does not demolish economics but distorts it through selfishness and greed. Sin does not destroy sexuality but diverts it down harmful paths. Sin does not do away with the need for politics but directs it to serve the interests of the powerful few. Small wonder that two of the most significant areas of our lives— work and family—can be a source of frustration as well as fulfilment; places of hurt as well as healing.

The disobedience of Eden results in disordered lives, and Genesis 4—11 describes how that disorder spreads like ripples from a stone thrown into a pond, moving through individuals to families to society to the whole of creation. And laced through these chapters, as God said it would be, is death.

It will take the next instalment of the story to show us that human rebellion and failure are met by God's grace, that God's commitment to his world and to humanity stands firm, that the way we are is not necessarily the way we will always be.

For further reflection and action

1. Where do you fall on the spectrum between 'naively optimistic' and 'overly pessimistic'? How does that affect your daily life and relationships?

2. Think about an experience from the last few days in which the tension of human existence in today's world was evident—a film you watched, a task you did, a conversation you had. How might we distinguish between a 'creational design' and something that has been distorted by the parasitic nature of sin?

3. Reflect on the significance of Matthew 18:22, where, echoing Lamech, Jesus commands extravagant forgiveness— 'not seven times, but seventy-seven times'.

*

Covenant

9: Restoration, restoration, restoration

The LORD had said to Abram, 'Go from your country, your people and your father's household to the land I will show you.

I will make you into a great nation,
and I will bless you;
I will make your name great,
and you will be a blessing.
I will bless those who bless you,
and whoever curses you I will curse;
and all peoples on earth
will be blessed through you.'

GENESIS 12:1–3

The downward spiral of rebellion in Genesis 3—11 is shot through with moments of God's mercy—in promising the destruction of the serpent, in providing coverings for Adam and Eve, in giving Cain a protective mark, in saving Noah and his family, in reaffirming God's blessing on creation and humanity after the flood. Even against the backdrop of the building of Babel by those who want to 'make a name' for themselves, judgment is not the last word: God does not reject the nations but chooses one family for the sake of the nations, to bring blessing to the nations.

That God does not leave us to our own devices is seen in the promise to Abraham, a threefold promise of restoration—

land, descendants and blessing. The guarantee of 'people' and 'land' shows the inseparability of who we are from where we find ourselves, both still crucial to human identity. Yet, even the assurance of a large family and a place for them to live is not the ultimate restoration. God's purpose (ratified in chapter 15, marked with the sign of circumcision in chapter 17, and repeated to Isaac and Jacob in the narratives that follow) is to mediate blessing to 'all peoples on earth', restoring humanity to its original purpose.

Thus begins the first episode in a long story, rooted in a people and a place, in which God progressively works out his plan of restoration. It will become clear as the story unfolds that all of human life, even creation itself, is included in its scope. In this way, God's promises to Abraham may be read in conjunction with Genesis 1—as a reaffirmation of his original blessing on men and women.

Covenants made between God and his people serve as major milestones in the biblical account, but the key that unifies them, and undergirds this covenant with Abraham, is the principle of promise. As Paul notes in Galatians 3:29, 'If you belong to Christ, then you are Abraham's seed, and heirs according to the promise.'

An inexpensive wine glass cracks and is thrown away. A rare vase breaks and is rebuilt, piece by piece, with precision and care, perhaps over a long period of time, until it is made whole again. Some broken things are restored because they're precious, because they are loved.

God remains, to this day, in the restoration business.

For further reflection and action

1. Think about the accounts that follow in the book of Genesis, moving from Abraham and Sarah through Isaac and Rebekah to Jacob and his family. From what you can recall of these stories, spend some time reflecting on how the promises God makes to Abraham appear to be threatened by all sorts of factors, except that God remains faithful, preserving the seed and working for good, even while others intend evil (Genesis 50:20). What significance might we draw from this for our own lives?

2. Follow up some references to Abraham in the New Testament (for example, Galatians 3:15–18; Romans 4:13–16; Hebrews 11:8–19). How are God's promises to Abraham ultimately fulfilled?

3. Think of 'broken' people and situations—in our own lives and the lives of others, in families, in churches, in workplaces and in countries across the world—and ask that the God who will one day 'bring all things in heaven and on earth together' (Ephesians 1:10, NIV) will provide a foretaste of that restoration to those in need.

10: Let my people go

The LORD said, 'I have indeed seen the misery of my people in Egypt. I have heard them crying out because of their slave drivers, and I am concerned about their suffering. So I have come down to rescue them from the hand of the Egyptians and to bring them up out of that land into a good and spacious land, a land flowing with milk and honey.'

EXODUS 3:7–8

Over 400 years had passed since Jacob's family took refuge in Egypt, when famine struck the eastern Mediterranean. Circumstances change, and his descendants eventually found themselves in slavery to the Egyptians. Did any of them hold on to the promise that God had given to Abraham, or keep in sight even the faintest vision of their destiny?

But God... All through the biblical story, the theme recurs: But God... The account of the exodus shows God as the director, with a cast of hundreds, each one of whom has to play their part. The Hebrew midwives and Moses' parents, then Pharaoh's daughter, ensure Moses' survival and his privileged position in Pharaoh's court. Then Moses takes centre stage and is given the unwelcome role of hero and deliverer. Even so, of course, the main actor in this drama is God himself; and, as Lord of heaven and earth, he demonstrates his power over the whole of creation—seen, not least, in the plagues, which represent an attack on Egyptian deities (see Exodus 12:12; Numbers 33:4).

On the last evening, when the final plague (the death of the firstborn sons) was to bring Pharaoh to his knees, the Israelites were given particular instructions: to prepare a meal of lamb, bitter herbs and bread without yeast, and to paint the lintels of their doors with the lambs' blood. Thus the feast of the Passover was instituted—when the destroyer 'passed over' the houses on which the blood was daubed—a feast that the Israelites were to celebrate as an annual remembrance, and which Jewish people have observed ever since.

The Passover calls to mind the sovereign call and redemptive action of God and the identity and destiny of his people. As his chosen people, they were to receive an inheritance and be a blessing to the world. That blessing finally reached out to the world at large only when God brought about his second great deliverance. 'Christ, our Passover lamb, has been sacrificed,' declared Paul (1 Corinthians 5:7), so that, as he reminded the Galatians (3:14), the blessing promised originally to Abraham might come to the Gentiles.

Thus, God's purpose for us, as his people today, is not simply that we might receive a blessing but that we might be agents of that blessing, wherever he has placed us.

For further reflection and action

1. The exodus is often seen as a foreshadowing of Christ's work of redemption on the cross. Spend some time thanking God for 'rescuing us from the dominion of darkness and bringing us into the kingdom of the Son he loves' (see Colossians 1:13).

2. Some Christians have used the exodus story as a model to seek liberation from political oppression. How legitimate is it to employ this one-off event in salvation history in support of political movements today?

3. How, today, might we bless others through our words and actions?

11: Two-way commitment

Then Moses went up to God, and the LORD called to him from the mountain and said, 'This is what you are to say to the descendants of Jacob and what you are to tell the people of Israel: "You yourselves have seen what I did to Egypt, and how I carried you on eagles' wings and brought you to myself. Now if you obey me fully and keep my covenant, then out of all nations you will be my treasured possession. Although the whole earth is mine, you will be for me a kingdom of priests and a holy nation." These are the words you are to speak to the Israelites.'

EXODUS 19:3–6

Three months out of Egypt, this ragbag collection of former slaves in the desert of Sinai reached a crucial moment in their history when the Lord began the process of forming a nation, fulfilling the promise he had made to Abraham and making a covenant with his people that resounds through the Bible. 'You are a chosen people, a royal priesthood, a holy nation, God's special possession', Peter told the scattered churches to whom he wrote (1 Peter 2:9), drawing on these words from Exodus.

This moment of life-changing commitment—like marriage or baptism or confirmation—involved preparation, formal promises before kin and community, and the knowledge that breaking the promises would have far-reaching consequences. So the people of Israel washed and refrained from sex, and the Lord came to them with thunder, lightning and thick cloud.

Then he said, 'I am the LORD your God, who brought you out of Egypt, out of the land of slavery. You shall have no other gods before me'—the beginning of the Ten Commandments (Exodus 20:2–3). Far from bringing about a new bondage, these commandments restored to the Israelites everything that slavery in Egypt had damaged and destroyed—freedom from pagan gods, freedom to work with dignity and take time off, freedom to maintain proper family relationships, freedom to construct a framework of law and order, freedom to own houses and livestock and to honour the ownership of others. The commandments were addressed in the singular to individuals in community, each one having the responsibility to maintain the conditions for all to flourish. And, since they had already been released from slavery, the commandments described the lifestyle of the redeemed, not the means of their redemption.

The calling to be a priestly kingdom, a holy nation, was a calling to be actively righteous, demonstrating the character of God to the world. The whole world is his, and his people were to be a light to the nations, serving only him. Yet none of the people standing before the mountain at Sinai would enter the land given to them; they would fail, and the rest of the Bible shows just how much failure there would be until God sent his Son as the Saviour of the world, beginning a new covenant.

For further reflection and action

1. The Ten Commandments have a somewhat poor reputation in today's society, although few can remember more than one or two of them. They're about 'don'ts', people say. Reflect on the commandments' positive encouragement to create societies of mutual support and flourishing.

2. Reflect on your covenant commitments to spouse, children, family and fellow Christians and, perhaps, repair some of the cracks.

3. Read Hebrews 12:18–29 and 2 Corinthians 3:7–18 for further reflections on the crucial significance of Sinai and its relationship to the glory of the new covenant.

12: Holy, holy, holy

The LORD said to Moses, 'Speak to the Israelites and say to them: "I am the LORD your God. You must not do as they do in Egypt, where you used to live, and you must not do as they do in the land of Canaan, where I am bringing you. Do not follow their practices. You must obey my laws and be careful to follow my decrees. I am the LORD your God. Keep my decrees and laws, for the person who obeys them will live by them. I am the LORD…"' The LORD said to Moses, 'Speak to the entire assembly of Israel and say to them: "Be holy because I, the LORD your God, am holy."'

LEVITICUS 18:1–5; 19:1–2

The life of the people of God is to reflect God's own character: 'Be holy because I, the LORD your God, am holy.'

The sheer range of regulations in Leviticus reminds us that the holiness in view touches all areas of life, not just the 'religious' ones; that holiness does not entail removal from the world but presupposes daily living in the world, as part of the rhythm of the week and the months, the cycle of the seasons; that holiness is not the preserve of the privileged few but is for all God's people; that holiness is not a privatised experience but is bound up with living and working in community.

Nor is holiness about floating free in some ethereal existence, untouched by the messiness of life. Rather, it is earthed (quite literally sometimes, on the ground) in everyday life—in working crops, maintaining soil, buying and selling goods; in looking after parents, observing sabbath rests and providing for the poor; in how one works, what one eats and who one sleeps with—consciously countering cultural norms in the process, living in the world but not living like the world.

All of this is carried out as an integral part of our worship of a holy God.

Lest we reduce the principle of holiness to an abstract system of laws, 'I am the LORD your God' reminds Israel that redemption comes before regulations, relationship before rules. The law is bound up with a commitment to serve their covenant Lord, to be a distinctive people and to order their lives with each other appropriately. And it is for the greater end of fulfilling God's promises to Abraham and the people's calling to be a priestly kingdom, for the sake of the world.

And lest we despair, knowing that the Israelites will never be able to live up to their calling, Leviticus assumes the reality and consequences of sin and makes provision for restoration through sacrifice.

Of course, the new covenant necessarily changes the dynamics and the specifics, but the vocation to be a people set apart for God remains (1 Peter 1:13–16; 2:9–10), and, with it, the call to do things differently from those around us. As we do so, we can expect that the laws will still shape our moral vision, because they arise out of God's holy character and express his mind for his people as we live in the face of the world for the sake of the world.

For further reflection and action

1. Read through the so-called 'Holiness Code' (Leviticus 18—20) and make a summary of the laws contained in it. Perhaps make a note of any surprises, and reflect on them further, alone or in conversation with others. Follow up the echoes of Leviticus in 1 Peter 1:13–16 and 2:9–10. How does Peter 'translate' holiness for the Christians to whom he writes?

2. What are some of the implications of the Old Testament law for a biblical worldview? Perhaps think personally about the implications for your own family life, business partnerships, leisure time, and so on.

3. How would you respond to someone who claimed that the laws in Leviticus are so buried in the culture of the time that they should be seen as of little or no value for today?

13: On the brink

Be strong and courageous, because you will lead these people to inherit the land I swore to their ancestors to give them. Be strong and very courageous. Be careful to obey all the law my servant Moses gave you; do not turn from it to the right or to the left, that you may be successful wherever you go.

JOSHUA 1:6–7

'Guide me, O Thou great Jehovah,' we sing, 'pilgrim through this barren land'; and we reach a climax of hope:

When I tread the verge of Jordan,
Bid my anxious fears subside:
Death of death and Hell's destruction
Land me safe on Canaan's side.
WILLIAM WILLIAMS (1745)

It may be comforting to think of crossing the River Jordan as death, and Canaan as heaven—except that the arrival of the Israelites in the land was not an end but a beginning. It was the beginning of the establishing of God's covenant people in God's promised land, living according to God's law in the midst of surrounding nations.

Here, then, was a fresh opportunity to serve the Lord. Moses had warned the people that God's blessing would remain with them only as long as they obeyed him. The law, with its emphasis on personal and communal holiness, was given to them for their flourishing, and to make them into a community committed to justice, generosity and stewardship, in a land where *each one* could live 'under their own vine and under their own fig tree' (1 Kings 4:25).

No wonder, then, with Canaan in sight on the other side of the Jordan, that God encourages Joshua to be strong and courageous: 'As I was with Moses, so I will be with you; I will never leave you nor forsake you' (Joshua 1:5).

Difficult though it might be for us to read accounts of the people of God wiping out the inhabitants of Canaan, the conquest of the land is not justified on ethnic grounds or because of Israel's moral superiority. Understood within the framework of God's justice, Israel's action against the Canaanites is portrayed as divine punishment for wicked acts (see Genesis 15:16; Deuteronomy 9:4–6; 12:29–31). The events also need to be seen within God's plan of salvation, which involves all nations, not just Israel: in fulfilment of his promise to Abraham, the Lord plants his people in a land where they can live under his rule, to be a blessing to the whole world.

As Williams' hymn testifies, the Old Testament narratives have been a rich source of imagery and inspiration to the church through the ages, perhaps none more so than the accounts of the exodus and the subsequent wanderings in the wilderness. For their part, New Testament writers understand these to be historical events, providing a pattern of how God both delivers his people and gives us 'rest' (Hebrews 3:7—4:13), and serving as examples and warnings to us (1 Corinthians 10:1–13).

Hence, as Christians today—God's new covenant people—we play our own part in God's unfolding drama. Redeemed by Christ and empowered by the indwelling Spirit, we are called to be God's new community in our own culture, with its particular temptations and dilemmas. And we too are to live righteously, strong and courageous, encouraged by the promise, 'I will never leave you nor forsake you.'

For further reflection and action

1. Reflect further on Joshua 1:8, with its call to meditate on God's law day and night, reminiscent of passages elsewhere in scripture (Deuteronomy 17:18–20; Psalm 1:2). How is the 'boldness' to which God calls us connected to our daily engagement with his word?

2. How can we, in our own circumstances, 'be strong and courageous' in upholding and maintaining the uniqueness and sovereign claims of God?

3. Is it more helpful to think of the Christian life as 'wandering in the wilderness' or 'living in the land'? How might your view find support from scripture?

14. Spiralling out of control

The Israelites did evil in the eyes of the LORD; they forgot the LORD their God and served the Baals and the Asherahs. The anger of the LORD burned against Israel so that he sold them into the hands of Cushan-Rishathaim king of Aram Naharaim, to whom the Israelites were subject for eight years. But when they cried out to the LORD, he raised up for them a deliverer, Othniel son of Kenaz, Caleb's younger brother, who saved them. The Spirit of the LORD came on him, so that he became Israel's judge and went to war. The LORD gave Cushan-Rishathaim king of Aram into the hands of Othniel, who overpowered him. So the land had peace for forty years, until Othniel son of Kenaz died. Again the Israelites did evil in the eyes of the LORD.
JUDGES 3:7–12

In the days when the judges ruled…
RUTH 1:1

Towards the end of his life, Joshua gathers the people together and recites the story of all that God has done for them. As he affirms that he and his household will serve the Lord, the people respond by saying that they too will stay faithful (Joshua 24:1–28).

Knowing our own capacity for self-delusion, however, we are perhaps not surprised to learn that, after Joshua's death, the people stray from the Lord. This leads into an era when there is no national leader or central government, with little unity between the tribes. Early military successes give way to failure, and moral apathy takes hold. Then, as now, neglect of the covenant relationship with God spills over into society.

Still, God doesn't abandon his people. They disobey him and he allows them to be defeated by enemies, but he responds to their cries for help by raising up a 'judge' through whom he brings deliverance—only for the people to turn away from him again. This pattern can be seen in the account of the first of these deliverers in Judges 3:7–12, but the cycle is repeated throughout the book.

If anything, the cycle becomes a downward spiral. The final chapters (Judges 17—21) portray the inevitable social breakdown in episodes of idolatry, lawlessness and civil war. The horrific story of the gang rape and dismemberment of a nameless woman (19:1–30) shocks us into realising how far the people of God have failed in their calling to be a holy nation, with everyone doing what is right in their own eyes (17:6). Alas, no judge arises to meet this progressive anarchy, and a recurring refrain—'Israel had no king' (17:6; 18:1; 19:1; 21:25)—strongly hints that something different is needed.

There is brutality, but there is also blessing. The first verse of the book of Ruth invites us to read the story that follows in the light of what we know of the period of judges. As we do so, the shameful, violent treatment of a woman gives way to tender, honourable conduct towards women. Through it all, the sovereign God works out his purpose with the inclusion of a Moabite 'outsider' into the fold of the covenant people—one who is not only, herself, a sign of the fulfilment of his promise to bless the nations, but from whom King David (Ruth 4:17–22) and Jesus himself (Matthew 1:1–5) are eventually born.

For further reflection and action

1. The judges were a mixed bunch of characters, themselves frequently flawed and fallible. What does this say about the kind of person God might use? How does the period of the judges help us long for a greater 'deliverer' who will bring a lasting solution to the problem of human rebellion?

2. Think about the resonances of the book of Judges with our contemporary situation in the West, where morality has arguably become largely a 'private' matter.

3. The book of Ruth shows how God works behind the scenes through ordinary events in everyday life. How far are you able to discern God's 'fingerprints' in the routine of your own life?

15: King for a day?

'The LORD declares to you that the Lord himself will establish a house for you: When your days are over and you rest with your ancestors, I will raise up your offspring to succeed you, your own flesh and blood, and I will establish his kingdom. He is the one who will build a house for my Name, and I will establish the throne of his kingdom forever. I will be his father, and he will be my son. When he does wrong, I will punish him with a rod wielded by men, with floggings inflicted by human hands. But my love will never be taken away from him, as I took it away from Saul, whom I removed from before you. Your house and your kingdom will endure forever before me; your throne will be established forever.'

2 SAMUEL 7:11B–16

Israel's struggle to take the land, and the destructive spiral of the period of the judges, pave the way for the monarchy. Thus begins the shift from a tribal society to a central government, where the focus of attention moves from the nation to the king.

With kingship comes the ambivalence of the political order and human rule that we know so well—its necessity alongside its tendency to corruption. The writers of the biblical records do not hide the negative details of Israel's kingship, the person of David included. But with kingship comes a further reminder of God's gracious willingness to get his fingers dirty with politics, society and culture; his determination to work through human foibles and failures; his ultimate oversight as the covenant relationship with his people is played out and preserved in the history and politics of real life.

At this point in the story, David has been crowned king, has defeated Israel's enemies and has moved the ark of the covenant to the newly secured capital city, Jerusalem. Concerned that his own royal palace is more lavish than God's dwelling, David is determined to build a temple for God. As it turns out, though, he is not allowed to build a 'house' (temple) for God, and instead is told that God will build a 'house' (dynasty) for him, giving him the promise of a kingdom that will last for ever, in which true kingship will be marked by faithfulness to God.

God's covenant with David adds a new dimension to the biblical story. Now we have a royal representative of the people—God's 'son', no less—with the promises of the covenant focused on Mount Zion, the place where God will be seen to dwell with his people as their true king. This language is echoed in many of the psalms, where the king's reign is celebrated as marked by wisdom and righteousness, providing a visible centre of God's rule for the sake of the nations.

As we might expect, then, God's commitment to David has implications beyond Israel and stands in continuity with the promise to Abraham of blessing to all nations, itself tied to God's purposes for creation. David and his sons will take centre stage in the story of God's dealings with men and women, so that through his line—through his anointed 'Son'—the Lord may restore and bless the whole world.

For further reflection and action

1. Resonances of 2 Samuel 7 are found in Psalms 2, 72, 89, 132; Isaiah 9:6–7; 11:1–5; Jeremiah 23:5–6; 33:14–26; Ezekiel 34:20–24. Pick a few of these passages to read. How do they fill out the details of what ideal 'kingship' should look like?

2. How does this passage illuminate our understanding of Jesus, descendant of David? Check out Luke 1:30–33; Acts 2:22–36; 13:32–36; Romans 1:2–4.

3. If possible, share and discuss with someone else the pattern we have seen in the biblical story so far, where there is a move from the 'particular' to the 'universal'. The Lord singles out one person (Abraham) for the blessing of the nations, and one nation (Israel) to be a light to the world, and now he singles out one king (David) and one place (Zion), for the sake of the extension of his rule to the ends of the world. In what ways is it possible to see Christians singled out in order to bless others? What examples of this have you seen in your own life?

16: The glory of the Lord filled the temple

When all the work King Solomon had done for the temple of the LORD was finished, he brought in the things his father David had dedicated—the silver and gold and the furnishings—and he placed them in the treasuries of the LORD's temple. Then King Solomon summoned into his presence at Jerusalem the elders of Israel, all the heads of the tribes and the chiefs of the Israelite families, to bring up the ark of the LORD's covenant from Zion, the City of David... The priests then brought the ark of the LORD's covenant to its place in the inner sanctuary of the temple, the Most Holy Place, and put it beneath the wings of the cherubim.

1 KINGS 7:51—8:1, 6

What a moment! The representatives of the people were gathered before the magnificent new temple. After the wars and rebellions of David's time, they were now safe in their kingdom, borders secured and enemies their vassals. Solomon, David's son, robed in splendour, supervised the journey of the ark of the covenant to the temple's Most Holy Place. This was a national and religious moment of joyful achievement and anticipation as the people of God worshipped the one true God in the house in which he dwelt, with psalms and sacrifices, living out their covenant commitment in their daily lives, the promises to Abraham and David fulfilled.

But this is not the beginning of a final renewed and perfect relationship between God and his people; we know what will happen. Solomon, despite all this glory, will break his covenant promises and lead the people astray. This picture of the temple, the place where God dwells and his people worship him, speaks of a truth more enduring than the physical bricks and stones that will be thrown down by Nebuchadnezzar and later, again, by the Romans.

This temple spoke of the unity of the people of God, together serving the one true God—no other place, no other gods, no idolatry, no syncretism. Even hundreds of miles away and many years later, when they were in exile, the picture of that central holy place, Jerusalem and the temple, held the love and commitment of God's faithful servants, dominating Ezekiel's prophetic visions and encouraging Daniel in his obedience to the Lord. Jesus himself, who foretold the temple's final destruction, said, 'Something greater than the temple is here' (Matthew 12:6), and Paul told the Corinthian church that *they* were God's temple, with God's Spirit living in them (1 Corinthians 6:19; 2 Corinthians 6:16).

The Bible ends with John's great vision of the new earth and the new heaven: 'I saw the Holy City, the new Jerusalem, coming down out of heaven from God... I did not see a temple in the city, the Lord God Almighty and the Lamb are its temple' (Revelation 21:2, 22). Significant as the temple is on the landscape of the biblical story, the final hope for God's people is the unmediated presence of God himself.

For further reflection and action

1. How would you describe your experience of 'sacred space'? Are there certain buildings (a church, a cathedral) or places (in the community, out in the countryside) that seem more 'holy' to you? If so, why might this be the case?

2. How far are our times together, singing and rejoicing and learning in church, an escape from outside realities, and how far are they a building up of our faith to serve the Lord more effectively from Monday to Saturday?

3. Think about how the 'temple' theme runs through the whole of scripture, from the garden of Eden to the city of the new Jerusalem. What stands at the heart of this theme?

17: Songs for all seasons

Praise the LORD, my soul;
all my inmost being, praise his holy name.
Praise the LORD, my soul,
and forget not all his benefits—
who forgives all your sins
and heals all your diseases,
who redeems your life from the pit
and crowns you with love and compassion,
who satisfies your desires with good things
so that your youth is renewed like the eagle's.
PSALM 103:1–5

In focusing on the extraordinary events in God's dealings with his people, we should not neglect the everyday faith of God's people, preserved in the psalms. These songs remind us that the story of salvation is not simply about what God has done in the past but is also the foundation for our ongoing relationship with him.

Of course, the psalms take their starting point from, and everywhere assume, the story of God's bond with his people. They make it clear that our whole life is bound up with his work as creator, redeemer, covenant maker and Torah giver, with the installation of his king on Mount Zion, and worship of him in the temple. These are not just songs of 'religious' people; these are songs of the covenant people of the Lord God.

Some of them, like Psalm 103, celebrate the Lord's rule in praise, declaring what he does for his people; and they allow us to add our worship to them. Others belong to the rawness of life, those moments when things fall apart—the redundancy notice, serious illness, the death of a spouse, relationship breakdown, yet another spat with the teenager of the house, those words said in anger, that difficult email, a news item that causes consternation or grief. They express with a powerful honesty what we might feel—awareness of guilt, loss of energy, a sense of rejection, protest at suffering, feelings of isolation, fear, helplessness, hurt, anger or rage. Many psalms also testify to God's grace in putting us back on track, not just to where we were but to somewhere different, a new place. And they do so in language which is poetic, imaginative, evocative and wide-ranging in its use of imagery.

In all of this, we are reminded that faith is not just content derived from scripture but a prayerful response to the God of scripture. The psalms hold together talk about God and talk addressed to God, and so they work not simply by matching our changing moods at any given time but by shaping the way we pray—collectively as well as individually—and shaping us in the process.

They do this because they are not finally about us but about God; not about the bricks and mortar of the temple, but the presence of God; not about King David, but the exercise of God's rule; not about following our own paths but about following the way of the covenant God.

For further reflection and action

1. What fresh insight, if any, does this reading contain, that will make a difference to the way you read and pray the psalms? From your own experience with the psalms, what important insight has the reading left unsaid?

2. Even a superficial glance through the psalms suggests that life will be interrupted, if not punctuated, by moments and periods of distress. Why do we struggle to incorporate this factor into church life, teaching and worship, and how might we begin to address it?

3. Take Psalm 103 or another one that is familiar to you, and try different ways of praying it. (1) Say it out loud, praying as you read; (2) read it, pausing now and then to add your own prayers to its lines; (3) paraphrase it, putting it into your own words; (4) pray through its possible implications for your week ahead; (5) commit it to memory over the course of a week.

18: Words for the wise

A wife of noble character who can find?
She is worth far more than rubies…
She selects wool and flax
and works with eager hands.
She is like the merchant ships,
bringing her food from afar…
She considers a field and buys it;
out of her earnings she plants a vineyard…

She opens her arms to the poor
and extends her hands to the needy...
She makes linen garments and sells them,
and supplies the merchants with sashes...
She speaks with wisdom,
and faithful instruction is on her tongue...
Charm is deceptive, and beauty is fleeting;
but a woman who fears the LORD is to be praised.
Honour her for all that her hands have done,
and let her works bring her praise at the city gate.
PROVERBS 31:10–31 (ABRIDGED)

The major turns in the biblical story—God's promise to Abraham, the redemption of Israel from slavery, the making of a covenant with the people, the giving of the law, the establishment of the monarchy, the building of the temple—are conspicuous by their absence in the biblical Wisdom literature.

As it turns out, wisdom is rooted further back—in creation, grounded in the orderly regulation of the world by the creator God, even with the acknowledgment (as Job and Ecclesiastes provide in different ways) that there are great mysteries woven into the fabric of life in God's world. Wisdom is not, therefore, a 'secular' alternative to other, more 'sacred' parts of the Bible. Nor is it surprising that Israel is able to engage with its surrounding cultures, gleaning insight where they reflect the truth that is God's truth, because of the recognition that he is the source of wisdom.

This is made clear in the opening of the book of Proverbs, where it is said that 'the fear of the LORD is the beginning of knowledge, but fools despise wisdom and instruction' (1:7). If Wisdom literature is concerned with living wisely in God's world, then fear of the Lord is the first principle of such a life, where wisdom does not begin in human autonomy but in deep reverence for the Lord God; where wisdom is not merely intellectual capacity but is linked with discipline and discernment, shrewdness and skill; where wisdom produces a certain kind of character and demonstrates itself in particular sorts of actions. What's more, wisdom operates in every sphere of life—at home, at the city gate, in the market square—and it embraces the daily rhythms of eating, drinking, working and sleeping.

These qualities are powerfully portrayed in the Bible's fullest description of the regular activity of an 'ordinary' person—the woman who 'fears the LORD' (31:30), whose wisdom is demonstrated in her everyday activities of being a wife to her husband and a mother to her children, providing for her family, managing her household, engaging in international trade in cloths and textiles, negotiating the purchase of fields and looking out for the poor.

Insofar as the woman is a picture of wisdom itself, matching the portrayal of 'Woman Wisdom' in earlier chapters of Proverbs (for example, 1:21–33; 8:1–36), the image is applicable to men as much as to women, setting out the ideal of practical wisdom, embracing actions and speech, worked out concretely in the kitchen, in the field or at the desk—wherever God has called us.

For further reflection and action

1. Read and reflect on the whole of Proverbs 31:10–31, perhaps pausing to consider how the 'fear of the Lord' might inform your own activities today.

2. From what you know of the Wisdom books of Job and Ecclesiastes, how do they balance out the more confident assertions found in the book of Proverbs about the way life tends to work?

3. Song of Songs is often held to belong to the Bible's Wisdom literature. What might this suggest about how the poems should be interpreted?

19: For the sake of David

When all Israel saw that the king refused to listen to them, they answered the king:
    'What share do we have in David,
    what part in Jesse's son?
    To your tents, Israel!
    Look after your own house, David!'

1 KINGS 12:16

It is 40 years since David's death. In spite of his achievements, Solomon's idolatry has brought God's judgment upon himself and upon the kingdom (1 Kings 11:9–13).

As the kingdom falls apart, we find ourselves asking, 'Who is in control?' Even before Solomon's death, Jeroboam is encouraged to rebel by a prophecy: 'I [God] am going to tear the kingdom out of Solomon's hand and give you ten tribes' (11:31). On his father's death, Solomon's son, Rehoboam, is crowned king. Jeroboam tries to strike a deal with him but is ruthlessly rejected. The Israelites respond with an immediate declaration of independence: 'To your tents, Israel! Look after your own house, David!' But this, we read, 'was from the

LORD, to fulfil the word the Lord had spoken to Jeroboam' (12:15).

Thus, the kingdom is divided, Jeroboam ruling the north (Israel) and Rehoboam the south (Judah). Both nations 'did evil in the eyes of the LORD', a refrain repeated throughout the chronicles of the kings, and both nations are ultimately judged—for the Bible never suggests that God's sovereignty nullifies human responsibility.

Israel, conquered by the Assyrians, was dispersed in 722BC, never to be restored, but the story of Judah was different. 'For the sake of my servant David,' God says, the southern kingdom will have a future (1 Kings 11:32–36). Even so, Judah's constant rebellion leads it too into exile, over a century later.

Yet the promise of return echoes through the declarations of the prophets. Ezekiel prophesies (37:15–28) that the Jews will return from exile as one nation, and 'my servant David will be king over them, and they will all have one shepherd' (v. 24). In spite of the return of Judah to Jerusalem, the true fulfilment of this prophecy begins with the coming of 'great David's greater Son' (as James Montgomery describes him in the hymn 'Hail to the Lord's Anointed', 1821). We might think of Jesus' words in John 10:16: 'I have other sheep that are not of this sheep pen. I must bring them also… and there shall be one flock and one shepherd.'

As it was for David's sake that God had mercy on Israel, so it is for Jesus' sake that he has mercy on us. Although we are responsible for working out our own salvation (Philippians 2:12), we cannot earn his favour: it is pure sovereign grace.

For further reflection and action

1. Thinking about the Israelites' repeated disobedience and its consequences, do we sometimes presume on God's grace? How do we understand the relationship between God's sovereignty and our responsibility in our own lives?

2. The people of the northern kingdom, Israel, who eventually returned from captivity, mingled and intermarried with the Assyrians and were called Samaritans, after their capital city, Samaria. From the Gospels we learn about the antagonism between Jews and Samaritans. What divisions of a historical, national, ethnic or religious nature impact our country and our churches?

3. Jesus said, 'Every kingdom divided against itself will be ruined' (Matthew 12:25). Do we too readily accept divisions in the global church and in our local churches today? What can we do about them?

20: Standing up and speaking out

The word of the LORD came to me, saying,

> 'Before I formed you in the womb I knew you,
> before you were born I set you apart;
> I appointed you as a prophet to the nations.'

… Then the LORD reached out his hand and touched my mouth and said to me, 'I have put my words in your mouth. See, today I appoint you over nations and kingdoms to uproot and tear down, to destroy and overthrow, to build and to plant.'

JEREMIAH 1:4–5, 9–10

From Moses to Malachi, from John the Baptist to John in Revelation, the prophets of the Bible brought God's words to his people. They were called by God to speak his words, interpreting events, challenging and confronting, predicting and warning, speaking for their own times, speaking for future times, speaking of Christ, speaking of the final day of the Lord.

The very name in which the prophets spoke—'Lord'—is the covenant name of God. On this basis they constantly reminded the people of God's commands against injustice and idolatry and his calls for social, economic and political righteousness, warning Israel and Judah of the judgment that would come, through foreign conquest and exile.

They challenged the rich and complacent: those who 'lie on beds adorned with ivory and lounge on [their] couches… who trample the needy and do away with the poor of the land' (Amos 6:4; 8:4). They challenged the priests and religious leaders: 'And now, you priests, this warning is for you. If you do not listen, and if you do not resolve to honour my name… I will send a curse on you… But you have turned from the way and by your teaching have caused many to stumble' (Malachi 2:1–2, 8). They challenged kings. Nathan confronted David: 'I anointed you king over Israel… Why did you despise the word of the LORD by doing what is evil in his eyes?' (2 Samuel 12:7–9). Elijah confronted Ahab: 'You have sold yourself to do evil in the eyes of the LORD… I am going to bring disaster on you' (1 Kings 21:20–21).

But with challenge came consolation, too. So it was that the prophets affirmed God's promises, looking forward to the day when Jerusalem's 'vindication shines out like the dawn, her salvation like a blazing torch' (Isaiah 62:1). They also spoke of grace and forgiveness. Through Jeremiah, the Lord says of his people that 'they will all know me, from the least of them to the greatest... For I will forgive their wickedness and will remember their sins no more' (31:34).

The prophets make it clear that the Lord acts in judgment and salvation for the sake of his people and for the ultimate blessing of the nations. Their message is of a piece with the rest of scripture—that if we are to enjoy relationship with God, it will not be based on our potential for improving ourselves but only because of his covenant love.

For further reflection and action

1. In Acts 2:17–18, Peter quoted the prophecy of Joel: 'In the last days... I will pour out my Spirit on all people. Your sons and daughters will prophesy... Even on my servants, both men and women, I will pour out my Spirit in those days, and they will prophesy.' Peter said this was happening on that very day of Pentecost. What role, if any, should prophecy have in the church today?

2. To what extent are Christians called, like the Old Testament prophets, to challenge religious leaders and political rulers when God's laws are flouted and when injustice and economic exploitation flourish? How do we recognise that call and support those who take on this role?

3. Read Isaiah 65:17–25 and Revelation 21:1–4, 22–27, and rejoice that in the end judgment is swallowed up in glory.

21: Loss and opportunity

The word came to Jeremiah concerning all the people of Judah… 'Because you have not listened to my words, I will summon all the peoples of the north and my servant Nebuchadnezzar king of Babylon,' declares the LORD, 'and I will bring them against this land and its inhabitants and against all the surrounding nations. I will completely destroy them and make them an object of horror and scorn, and an everlasting ruin… This whole country will become a desolate wasteland, and these nations will serve the king of Babylon seventy years. But when the seventy years are fulfilled…'

JEREMIAH 25:1, 8–9, 11–12

Destruction of cities, despoliation of land, deportation of people. Then, as now, whole nations were vulnerable to military defeat.

Jeremiah declares the end game in the slow decline of the southern kingdom of Judah (the northern kingdom having been laid waste 150 years earlier), with a series of invasions by Babylon, culminating in the death blow of 586BC, when Jerusalem fell, the temple and royal palace were destroyed, and much of the population was forcibly removed.

Aside from the geographical dislocation and political breakdown involved, the exile was an upheaval that shook the foundations of the very existence of God's people, calling into question major sources of significance—the land that God had promised Abraham; the throne of David that would last for ever; the city of Zion that would never fall; the temple of the Lord, his dwelling-place, along with its priesthood and sacrificial apparatus. All were reduced to rubble.

Small wonder that the exile forced deep reflection about matters of identity, grounds of hope, reasons for suffering and symbols of faith. What had gone wrong? Was the Lord too weak? Or had he given up on his promises? Was there any future for the people of Israel?

Small wonder, too, that they responded in ways that disclose the intensity of the grieving experience: shock, anger, denial, guilt, nostalgia, acceptance. In fact, a substantial portion of the Old Testament writings flows out of the exile, reflecting different dimensions and articulating different responses—cries of lament, curses against enemies, expressions of doubt, protests of innocence and pleas for forgiveness—all directed to God. The common thread that runs through these responses is that although judgment comes from him, it will not be his last word: he remains committed to the covenant and his people.

It is sometimes said that churches today find themselves in a situation akin to 'exile', largely without privilege, no longer enjoying broad support, in an environment that is indifferent or hostile. But, as Israel's history demonstrates, in God's providence a time of exile can prove rich and fertile, where God's people can live out an alternative lifestyle within the dominant culture, which doesn't involve repudiating the culture. On the contrary, exiles who 'seek the peace and prosperity of the city' (Jeremiah 29:7) find their vocation in the here and now of the contemporary world, in the 'secular' sphere where the church must necessarily live.

Christian identity and mission are forged in the crucible of exile.

For further reflection and action

1. Read 2 Kings 25, the historical description of what was prophesied by Jeremiah.

2. 'Cries of lament, curses against enemies, expressions of doubt, protests of innocence and pleas for forgiveness.' When things go wrong, which response—if any—is your default mode, and why?

3. Jeremiah's letter to the exiles in chapter 29 calls on them to 'seek the peace and prosperity of the city' (29:7) to which they have been carried in exile. What might that look like for 'exiles' in the contemporary world? In what concrete ways might you be able to do it today?

22: Peril and providence

'Go, gather together all the Jews who are in Susa, and fast for me… When this is done, I will go to the king, even though it is against the law. And if I perish, I perish.'

ESTHER 4:16 (ABRIDGED)

'If we are thrown into the blazing furnace, the God we serve is able to deliver us from it, and he will deliver us from Your Majesty's hand. But even if he does not, we want you to know, Your Majesty, that we will not serve your gods or worship the image of gold you have set up.'

DANIEL 3:17–18

Keeping his head as a young student enrolled in the university of Babylon, Daniel learned quickly when and how the line between integrity and compromise had to be drawn in the sands of exile. Likewise, for the young queen Esther, married to the most powerful king in the world (a man possessed of a violent temper and a poor track record in married life), there came a time when a stand had to be taken and her identity as one of God's people declared.

Is it any easier for young Christians today, when parental restraint and church ties can so easily be traded in for the perceived freedom outside the Christian bubble? Negotiating that line between serving the Lord and serving Nebuchadnezzar—or Christ and Caesar—doesn't get easier as life goes on. Workplaces inevitably have their own culture and set of values, where identity can be shaped every bit as overtly and covertly as it was for Daniel and Esther.

Yet, with Daniel, 'they could find no corruption in him, because he was trustworthy and neither corrupt nor negligent'. Even those plotting against him said, 'We will never find any basis for charges against this man Daniel unless it has something to do with the law of his God' (6:4–5). For all their jealousy, his detractors knew that he was not some ambitious young careerist, hacking his way up the administrative ladder. They had the wit to see that what made him tick was his central motivation to serve God.

Like other captives, Daniel and Esther had to wrestle with God's purpose for their lives. Back home, the mandate to be a light to the nations, a kingdom of priests for the sake of the world (Exodus 19:6), could be a distant implication of their calling. Now conquered and carried off into the world beyond, the question was whether they would learn the lessons of exile and trust the God who went before them.

In exile—as in universities, workplaces and homes today —God's people are not called to a leisure-time faith, which might affect their private life but have no impact on the public world. Esther and Daniel were, no doubt, both tempted to wonder if the reach of the God of Israel extended into the hostile world in which they lived. Yet, hundreds of miles from the temple in Jerusalem, they gained a grander vision of their God.

For further reflection and action

1. Imagine: Daniel and his fellow exiles would probably have been marched as captives into the capital city of the Babylonian superpower through the imposing Ishtar Gate (14 metres high and 30 metres wide) and would have been confronted by a city more advanced in architecture and technology than any in the world at that time, with displays of military victory and imperial ideology at every turn. Think about your own context today and the places where you see evidence of superior might and values.

2. How did the exile challenge and change Israel's vision of her covenantal God?

3. If you sense that your friends and colleagues are content in their lack of interest in God, or even resolved in their dismissal of him, remember that 'Christ plays in ten thousand places' (Gerard Manley Hopkins), and, as the psalmist says, 'Where can I go from your Spirit? Where can I flee from your presence?' (Psalm 139:7). Ask God for eyes to see him at work in their lives, and for wisdom to

pick up on conversations with the tact and boldness that Esther and Daniel possessed.

23: All change

'I will take you out of the nations; I will gather you from all the countries and bring you back into your own land. I will sprinkle clean water on you, and you will be clean; I will cleanse you from all your impurities and from all your idols. I will give you a new heart and put a new spirit in you; I will remove from you your heart of stone and give you a heart of flesh. And I will put my Spirit in you and move you to follow my decrees and be careful to keep my laws. Then you will live in the land I gave your ancestors; you will be my people, and I will be your God.'

EZEKIEL 36:24–28

Even while the exile takes its toll, warnings of judgment give way to promises of restoration. Under God's direction, the prophets who addressed the people with words of condemnation now bring words of comfort. They do so in order to provide hope where there is no hope, and reassurance where there is remorse; and they do so in terms that the people will understand.

Thus it is that Jeremiah, Ezekiel and Isaiah between them envisage a return to the land, a return that will be a replay of the exodus, as God's people come back home. They will benefit from the wise reign of a king from the line of David, who will be a good shepherd to them. The temple will be restored, with everything in its place and God himself once again dwelling with his people.

But something more fundamental than land, kingship and temple is required. At the heart of God's promises is the restoration of the people themselves—an inward renewal, which God himself will bring about, as he pledges to cleanse his people and give them a new heart and a new Spirit. The fact that this is nothing less than a resurrection is confirmed to Ezekiel in a powerful vision, showing how God can bring piles of dry bones together, put flesh on them and breathe his Spirit into them, just as he did with Adam at creation.

The words 'You will be my people, and I will be your God' (v. 28) express in a concise formula the covenant between God and his people; Jeremiah likewise sees the goal of restoration to be a re-establishment of the covenant relationship, with a new covenant written on the heart (31:31–34). This is an internal rather than external reality, available to all.

Of course, with restoration will come recommitment and responsibility—to be the servant community, a light for the nations. No wonder the final chapters of Isaiah envisage not just the rebuilding of Jerusalem, but a city filled with the glory of God that finds itself at the centre of a new heaven and a new earth—reminding us once again that the prophets hold out a vision of hope not just for the people of God but for the nations as well; and not just for the nations but for the whole of creation.

How good is the God we adore!

For further reflection and action

1. Given the very specific context in which this promise of restoration is given, how far is it legitimate to use the words of Ezekiel to convey hope today? What sorts of contemporary situations might count?

2. From the period of exile flow predictions of judgment, cries of lament, pleas for forgiveness, instructions to build, warnings of persecution, promises of restoration, and more. Think about when it might be appropriate to take up these different types of language in prayer, and draw on them this week as you read magazines, watch the news on TV or engage with colleagues, or as you reflect on your local church situation or the place you're at in your own walk with God.

3. Other promises about restoration speak of a coming figure who is described variously as a 'shepherd king', a 'servant of the Lord', and one 'like a Son of Man'. Think about how these resonances carry through to the New Testament, where they inform Jesus' understanding of himself and his mission.

24: Rebuilding walls, rebuilding lives

When the LORD restored the fortunes of Zion,
we were like those who dreamed.
Our mouths were filled with laughter,
our tongues with songs of joy.
Then it was said among the nations,
'The LORD has done great things for them.'
The LORD has done great things for us,
and we are filled with joy.

PSALM 126:1–3

'The Return' is one of the great themes of history and literature, and nowhere is it more clearly written than in the return of the Judeans to Jerusalem after 70 years in captivity.

But it was only when Babylon was superseded by Persia that the time of release finally came.

Cyrus was an enlightened ruler who followed a policy of 'multiculturalism' throughout his empire. Prompted by God, he proclaimed the release of as many Jews as wished to leave, to rebuild the temple in Jerusalem. Unlike many other 'returns' of refugees or exiles, whose first concern is to find their families and homes and retrieve their possessions, this first return was focused on the temple.

The Jewish people's relationship with God was intrinsic to their identity. It was expressed in terms of place—the land, the city, the temple. The land had been lost and the buildings destroyed, but, when the time came to return, the first opportunity granted to them was to reinstate the worship of God at the centre of their corporate life. Despite opposition, the temple was completed in 20 years, amid great rejoicing. However, it wasn't until 60 years later that Ezra, 'a teacher well versed in the Law of Moses' (Ezra 7:6), led a further wave of immigration. Once again, the main emphasis was on the temple and its worship, but Ezra was also given administrative and civil authority.

Nevertheless, the walls and gates of the city were still in ruins, and it fell to Nehemiah, a decade or so later, to organise the rebuilding. As we read his story, we are able to see how the restoration of God's people involved 'practical' matters (for example, rebuilding the broken Dung Gate in the city wall, Nehemiah 3:14) as well as 'spiritual' matters (such as confessing sin, 9:1–3). In all these tasks, Ezra and Nehemiah were conscious of the 'hand of the Lord' (Ezra 7:6, 28) over their plans and actions.

The people likewise entered into the vision of their leaders, flinging themselves wholeheartedly into the building projects.

The walls were finished, houses rebuilt and towns resettled. When all the work was completed, they asked Ezra to bring out the Book of the Law of the Lord, and, as they listened, understood and responded to it, they recognised that the restoration of their community rested on the restoration of their relationship with God.

For further reflection and action

1. What is your equivalent of 'rebuilding the broken Dung Gate' today, and how will you serve God through it?

2. How might the church take the lead in challenging the sacred–secular divide in society today?

3. Read Nehemiah 8—9 and reflect on the role of scripture (including the telling of the biblical story, no less!) in shaping the renewal of God's people.

25: A partial restoration

You have wearied the LORD with your words. 'How have we wearied him?' you ask. By saying, 'All who do evil are good in the eyes of the LORD, and he is pleased with them' or 'Where is the God of justice?' 'I will send my messenger, who will prepare the way before me. Then suddenly the Lord you are seeking will come to his temple; the messenger of the covenant, whom you desire, will come,' says the LORD Almighty. But who can endure the day of his coming? Who can stand when he appears? … Surely the day is coming; it will burn like a furnace…' says the LORD Almighty. 'Not a root or a branch will be left to them. But

for you who revere my name, the sun of righteousness will rise
with healing in its rays.'
MALACHI 2:17–3:2; 4:1–2 (ABRIDGED)

Still disobedient, still wearying the Lord, the exiles found
that their return had only partially fulfilled the promises to
Abraham, Moses and David. There was a measure of return,
a measure of rebuilding—temple and walls—a measure of
restoration for Jerusalem and her people. Yet even as Ezra
led the worship in the newly built temple, would they have
recalled in their hearts the great days of David and Solomon,
when their kingdom was powerful and prosperous, the envy
of their neighbours? And that first generation back from exile,
would they not have remembered the Jews left behind in
Babylon and the graves of those who had died there? Would
they not have looked at the neglected villages and fields and
the strangers living around them with little knowledge of the
Lord God? Might they have wondered when other conquerors
would come?

There must have been great joy as they sang God's praises
in a rebuilt temple and city. But just as their joy was tinged
with some regret, some sadness, some sense of repentance
that their ancestors had brought it on themselves, so is all
human joy tempered. Whether it's love in relationships or
beauty in art, music and nature, or whether it's seeing health
restored, a degree of justice delivered or some of the hungry
fed, our joys are tempered by the partial nature of all good
things.

For them and for us, these glimpses of joy are heralds
of promise—that one day all the promises of God will be
fulfilled and joy will be complete. Malachi looked forward to
the day when the Lord's messenger would come and prepare

the way for the sun of righteousness with healing in his rays—the Lamb, the Saviour and Redeemer. That Redeemer would come, as a man, to this earth as it is, with its broken walls and ruined cities, exiled people, conquerors and conquered. And his death and resurrection would speak of eternity in place of fleeting time. It will be a promise fulfilled for us, who wait for the day of his final coming as judge and king, when we shall see the glory of a world made young again, death defeated and his kingdom complete in a new Jerusalem.

For further reflection and action

1. Read Isaiah 60. See how the images of land, exile and return are used to express God's promises of restoration and salvation. The chapter also speaks of God's people as a light and beacon, to which peoples and nations flock not as enemies but as suppliants and gift-bearers. How might these images apply to the church today?

2. Our personal life experiences are often a complicated mixture of joy and sadness. How far is this reality reflected in the music we listen to, the books we read, the films we watch and the way we view the world in which we live?

3. In the next reading, we move into the New Testament. Jesus was born into all the ambiguities and messiness of a nation ruled by puppet-kings and priests under Roman conquerors. Some would see John the Baptist as the messenger promised by Malachi, and Jesus as the Messiah. Others would oppose both John and Jesus. Reflect on the continuity here with the return from exile—and with the position of the church today.

Christ

26: The key to scripture

[Jesus] said to them, 'How foolish you are, and how slow to believe all that the prophets have spoken! Did not the Messiah have to suffer these things and then enter his glory?' And beginning with Moses and all the Prophets, he explained to them what was said in all the Scriptures concerning himself... When he was at the table with them, he took bread, gave thanks, broke it and began to give it to them. Then their eyes were opened and they recognised him, and he disappeared from their sight. They asked each other, 'Were not our hearts burning within us while he talked with us on the road and opened the Scriptures to us?' They got up and returned at once to Jerusalem.

LUKE 24:25–27, 30–33

As we move from the old covenant scriptures to the new covenant scriptures, this short but compelling scene provides a lens through which to view the whole story. It also captures suggestive truths about our engagement with God through his word.

The first resurrection day sees Cleopas and a companion (possibly his wife) walking back home from Jerusalem to their village, Emmaus. Jesus joins them on the road and asks about their discussion. They are able to summarise what has happened and to do so accurately, but they fail to understand its significance. 'We *had* hoped that he was the one...' (24:21) expresses their sense of loss and disillusionment. What can make sense of it?

Interestingly, they needed more than just an experience of the resurrected Christ. Note that Jesus does not say to them, 'How foolish you are, and how slow to believe that I have risen.' Nor does he say, 'How foolish you are, and how slow to believe all that I have spoken.' He says, 'How foolish you are, and how slow to believe all that the prophets have spoken.' He takes them back to the scriptures, in a way that shows how the scriptures make sense of the situation in which they find themselves. And he does so in such a way that, as they say afterwards, their hearts burned within them while he talked (v. 32).

We're not told what he said, although Luke—like the other Gospel writers—provides some pointers, showing how the significance of Jesus' own story is not found in isolated passages here and there but is woven into the larger story of creation and covenant, of Abraham and Moses, of David and Jerusalem, of law and monarchy, of priesthood and temple, of visions of restoration beyond exile. For us, it is a reminder that Jesus cannot be understood apart from the Old Testament, and the Old Testament cannot be understood apart from Jesus.

Even so, the moment of full recognition awaits the fellowship at the table, alluding back to the last supper and the reminder that God's purposes would be carried out through suffering and death, so that sins could be forgiven and the covenant renewed.

It's perhaps no surprise, then, that the result of all this is the compelling need to tell others! Engagement with scripture and the story it tells, which has come to its culmination in Christ, results in the ongoing transformation of disciples as hearts burn within, as eyes are opened and as feet are energised to pass on the good news.

For further reflection and action

1. Reflect on moments in your life when scripture (a) has made sense of a situation you have been facing, (b) has given you fresh insights about Jesus, and (c) has motivated you to tell others about Jesus.

2. Read the next episode, in Luke 24:36–49, noting the similar moments when Jesus comes to a group of disciples in need, explains scripture to them, makes himself known to them in fellowship and inspires them to tell others.

3. In Luke 24:47, Jesus' explanation of scripture includes the dimension that 'repentance for the forgiveness of sins will be preached in his name to all nations, beginning at Jerusalem'. Try to discuss with someone else this 'all nations' aspect of the biblical story, how Jesus brings about the fulfilment of God's plan for the nations and what it might mean for disciples of Christ living in today's world.

27: The Word became flesh

In those days Caesar Augustus issued a decree that a census should be taken of the entire Roman world... So Joseph also went up from the town of Nazareth in Galilee to Judea, to Bethlehem the town of David, because he belonged to the house and line of David. He went there to register with Mary, who was pledged to be married to him and was expecting a child. While they were there, the time came for the baby to be born, and she gave birth to her firstborn, a son. She wrapped him in cloths and placed him in a manger, because there was no guest room available for them.

LUKE 2:1, 4–7

It's such an ordinary story—government orders, people on the move, a baby born in a mucky corner of a third world city to a not-yet-married mother. We know the story, 'celebrated' in tinsel and pictures of reindeer from Tokyo to Timbuktu, from San Francisco to Seoul. And this one ordinary baby has had influence beyond anyone else, born before or since— with millions counting their years and their history from his birth, millions knowing his name, one way or another.

Matthew ties Jesus' birth into the Old Testament story: 'fourteen generations in all from Abraham to David, fourteen from David to the exile to Babylon, and fourteen from the exile to the Messiah' (1:17). The songs in Luke 1—2 also have deep roots in promises of old, celebrating God's grace in bringing about the fulfilment of his covenant with Abraham. The birth of this child signifies the end of pain for humanity, the presence of God in mercy, the coming of the golden age. John reaches further back, to the very dawn of all things: 'In the beginning was the Word, and the Word was with God, and the Word was God… Through him all things were made… the Word became flesh and made his dwelling among us' (1:1, 3, 14).

The Word became flesh. This pivotal point in all history— the history of our world, of creation, of the universe; the history of humans, from the moment when they are made in the image of their creator, through the Fall, and to the end of time—comes with the birth of one small, vulnerable, helpless human being, whose significance and uniqueness have unimaginable implications for you and for me.

This intertwining of the mundane and the marvellous continues as we read through the four Gospels. We experience a gradual unveiling as we follow the contours of Jesus' story, as we begin to understand who he is and what he comes to do. We rejoice that this man, our Lord and Saviour, understands what it means to be human, vulnerable and subject to thirst and weariness, pain and death. We rejoice in all the promises of salvation, forgiveness, mercy and grace won for us on the cross. And we rejoice that he rose from the dead and promises that resurrection to us too—'born to raise the sons of earth, born to give them second birth' (Charles Wesley, 1739).

For further reflection and action

1. Can you look back and see evidence of God working in your life before you asked him to be in it?

2. 'The Word of God' sounds throughout the Bible. Reflect on the biblical background behind the use of the word 'Word' in John's first chapter. Look at Genesis 1:3, where God speaks, and it happens, and at Revelation 22:20, where he speaks again: 'Yes, I am coming soon.' In what ways has God spoken to you in the past week?

3. Reflect on the cultural traditions of Christmas as practised in your household and your part of the world. How far should Christians challenge or affirm aspects of the popular patterns of this 'celebration'?

28: The Lord reigns

After John was put in prison, Jesus went into Galilee, proclaiming the good news of God. 'The time has come,' he said. 'The kingdom of God has come near. Repent and believe the good news!'

MARK 1:14–15

'The kingdom of God has come near.' That's the summary of Jesus' message when he bursts on to the scene in Galilee. What was he talking about? What is the 'kingdom of God' or the 'kingdom of heaven' (Matthew's preferred phrase)?

The first thing to note is that the kingdom of God is not primarily a place—the place where God lives or the place we go to when we die. Instead, when we read of the 'kingdom', we should think of the kingship of God, the exercise of his royal rule. Jesus was effectively saying that God was at last beginning to reign.

It's not that he wasn't king already, of course! But the Jews of Jesus' time were living under foreign rule, and had been for centuries. If Israel were truly God's people, why were pagans ruling them? They might well be back in their land, but it was almost as if they were still in exile. They were certainly still waiting for God to act on their behalf, to step in and exercise his full kingship. And Jesus announces the good news that that time has now come.

So whenever Jesus exercised the authority of God, he was putting down a marker for the kingdom. 'If it is by the Spirit of God that I drive out demons', he argued, 'then the kingdom of God has come upon you' (Matthew 12:28). Such events were a foretaste of the victory that Jesus won over Satan by his death and resurrection, when, 'having disarmed the powers and authorities, he made a public spectacle of them, triumphing over them by the cross' (Colossians 2:15). The final establishment of the kingdom, of course, awaits Jesus' return, 'when he hands over the kingdom to God the Father after he has destroyed all dominion, authority and power' (1 Corinthians 15:24).

Where does this leave us, living as we do between Jesus' resurrection and his final triumph? We are called, as his followers, to proclaim the kingdom and live out its values as 'salt of the earth' and 'light of the world' (Matthew 5:13–14). Proclaim and live out—a double challenge. In an age desperately in need of values to live by, we are called to speak up for the values of the kingdom—for integrity, truthfulness and compassion. Then, we seek to live by these values in our families, communities and workplaces, proclaiming by our lives that God reigns.

For further reflection and action

1. 'Your kingdom come, your will be done, on earth as it is in heaven' (Matthew 6:10). What might it mean for you, in your particular situation, to pray this prayer today?

2. Here's something to mull over, perhaps with another Christian: what is the relationship between the 'kingdom' and the 'church'?

3. As a citizen of the kingdom, an ambassador for Christ, where is your 'frontline' (the place where you spend most of your time in an ordinary week)? How, at this point,

can you seek to challenge prevailing attitudes and ways of doing things, and seek to recommend kingdom values?

29: Apostles and apprentices

As Jesus was walking beside the Sea of Galilee, he saw two brothers, Simon called Peter and his brother Andrew. They were casting a net into the lake, for they were fishermen. 'Come, follow me,' Jesus said, 'and I will send you out to fish for people.' At once they left their nets and followed him. Going on from there, he saw two other brothers, James son of Zebedee and his brother John. They were in a boat with their father Zebedee, preparing their nets. Jesus called them, and immediately they left the boat and their father and followed him.

MATTHEW 4:18–22

It was normal for those who wanted to follow a teacher to choose for themselves who they would follow. Instead, though, Jesus takes the initiative in calling the disciples—and when he calls, they respond.

Luke tells us that Jesus spent a night praying on a mountainside before he named the men who were to be his special disciples, or apostles (Luke 6:12–13). He had called them to be with him for the three years or so of his public ministry. He called twelve, and the Gospel writers carefully record their names (Matthew 10:2–4; Mark 3:16–19; Luke 6:14–16). These twelve men, recalling the twelve tribes of Israel, would be the messengers of the kingdom to the world, the planters of the church, the foundation stones of the restored people of God. In his vision of the new creation, John sees their names on the twelve foundations of the wall of the new Jerusalem, the Holy City, just as the names of the twelve tribes of Israel are written on the gates (Revelation 21:12, 14).

Jesus taught the disciples, involving them in his ministry and sending them out to proclaim the good news of the kingdom. But the powerful symbolism of the number twelve does not mean that these men were the only disciples: Jesus once sent out 72 on a mission (Luke 10:1). Some of the twelve hardly figure at all in the narrative. Of the ones we do read about, we see them learning from him, sometimes doubting and misunderstanding him, sometimes questioning his decisions. But we also see them realising the amazing truth about the Lord who had called them.

'You will be my witnesses,' Jesus told them, just before his ascension (Acts 1:8). As we read the book of Acts and the letters of the apostles, we see them laying the foundations of the church by their teaching and preaching, and we ourselves are grafted into the body of Christ, his church, through their teaching.

We too are Jesus' disciples. God's reign has at last broken into the world to bring salvation and renewal. As part of that larger reality, men and women are graciously called by Jesus ('Come, follow me...') and then commissioned by Jesus ('and I will send you out to fish for people'). For us, as for them, discipleship is apprenticeship in the work of the kingdom, learning from Jesus and learning with others.

For further reflection and action

1. By calling twelve apostles, Jesus was reminding the early Jewish Christians of their heritage as the people of Israel, the people of God. With today's multiplicity of churches,

new and old, how far is it important for Christians to know their heritage, honouring the Christian past and the history of the church?

2. There is much reassurance in the story of Jesus and his disciples. He chose the imperfect, the doubters and the muddle-headed, but he trusted them to do his work in his world, empowered by the Holy Spirit. How might we use this as a model for the way we encourage our employees, our children and our fellow believers?

3. 'Discipleship is apprenticeship in the work of the kingdom, learning from Jesus and learning with others.' Based on your reading or knowledge of the Gospels, put together a list of the characteristic marks of discipleship.

30: In word and deed

Jesus went throughout Galilee, teaching in their synagogues, proclaiming the good news of the kingdom, and healing every disease and sickness among the people. News about him spread all over Syria, and people brought to him all who were ill with various diseases, those suffering severe pain, the demon-possessed, those having seizures, and the paralysed; and he healed them. Large crowds from Galilee, the Decapolis, Jerusalem, Judea and the region across the Jordan followed him.

MATTHEW 4:23–25

Matthew summarises here what he describes more fully elsewhere, and what the other Gospel writers also make clear—that the story of Jesus cannot be presented without telling of his acts of power and compassion, healing and transformation.

The ancient world had its fair share of 'healers', but Jesus was different—and people knew it. Not only does the list of those healed emphasise the authority of Jesus over all kinds of sickness, but his healings are a sign that, after years of seeming silence, God's saving rule is now beginning to dawn in Israel. In words and in works, Jesus is proclaiming nothing less than the arrival of God's reign, announcing and enacting the presence and power of the kingdom—bringing sight to the blind, hearing to the deaf, mobility to the lame, even life to the dead.

In the exorcisms, individuals oppressed in different ways are freed, signalling a defeat for the powers of darkness. Their deliverance—not by any magical means but by a rebuke and a command—marks the presence of the kingdom. Where those with skin diseases of various kinds are socially ostracised, Jesus breaks taboos by stepping outside the 'circle of purity' in order to rescue them, not only making them whole but reintegrating them into the community. All of this shows that the works of the kingdom are not just an exercise of bare power but an expression of covenant love—bringing liberation and renewal, touching the whole of our lives, reconstituting the people of God.

In his nature miracles, too (for example, the calming of the storm, the multiplication of loaves and fishes), Jesus demonstrates the good news he proclaims, that God's rule over all creation—not just Israel—is being exercised. His works reveal in advance something of God's purposes for the restoration of the whole created order, offering us glimpses of a renewed cosmos from which the powers of darkness will be ejected, when sickness and pain will be no more, and God's creation will be restored to its original harmony.

Within the context of the Gospels—and as the letters of Paul and others will make clear—victory is bound up with the work that Jesus will do on the cross and in his resurrection. Meanwhile, as we look forward to the final redemption that will come to every part of creation, we delight that no area of the world is beyond God's reach, no aspect of life exempt from his rule.

For further reflection and action

1. Read about some of Jesus' works of healing and deliverance in Matthew 8—9.

2. Jesus proclaimed the coming of the kingdom not only with words but with deeds of power. How far can we be faithful to his teaching without acknowledging the place of healing and casting out demons? Dare we exclude the possibility of miracles today?

3. Even so, God usually works in normal ways through normal means. Reflect on the everyday ways in which you see God at work in your own life and in the lives of others.

31: He came to his own...

Jesus returned to Galilee in the power of the Spirit, and news about him spread through the whole countryside. He was teaching in their synagogues, and everyone praised him. He went to Nazareth, where he had been brought up, and on the Sabbath day he went into the synagogue, as was his custom. He stood up to read, and the scroll of the prophet Isaiah was handed to him. Unrolling it, he found the place where it is written:

'The Spirit of the Lord is on me,

because he has anointed me

to proclaim good news to the poor.

He has sent me to proclaim freedom for the prisoners

and recovery of sight for the blind,

to set the oppressed free,

to proclaim the year of the Lord's favour.'

LUKE 4:14–19

It was an ordinary sabbath, with the people of Nazareth in the synagogue together—except, that day, a young man they knew, the son of a local carpenter, had returned to the town. They had heard widespread praise of his teaching in other parts of Galilee and now he was in their synagogue, reading from Isaiah 61.

In its first setting, the figure of Isaiah 61 comes to the downtrodden people of God in exile. He is commissioned by God, anointed with the Spirit, and comes to announce that comfort and salvation are close at hand.

And then Jesus said, 'Today this scripture is fulfilled in your hearing' (Luke 4:21).

Here at this local event in the local synagogue, Jesus spoke to the people and they responded. At first they spoke well of him, pleased with the success of a local man, looking forward to seeing some miracles, perhaps. But he continued to speak, challenging them to see that just as Israel had rejected the prophets, so the people of his home town would not understand him. As Elijah and Elisha had gone beyond Israel to the Gentiles to perform their miracles, so the Jewish people of Jesus' day would find that God's kingdom would extend to bless the poor, the prisoner, the outcast and the Gentile. This was too much for the people of Nazareth, and they became so angry that they tried to kill him (v. 29).

Here and in many more passages, the Gospel writers report Jesus' challenges to Israel, especially to her leaders. They were waiting for the restoration of the Davidic kingdom, for a proper and complete return from exile, for a Messiah who would throw out the Gentile conquerors, reinstate Israel's ancient borders, restore her ethnic purity and enforce her laws. Jesus, Israel's true Messiah, challenged them to a different agenda—to seek the lost sheep, take back the repentant sons, care for the widows and orphans, welcome the alien and stranger, demonstrate to the world the love and mercy of their God, and recognise his Lordship. He challenged them to look at their own history and to open their ears to the prophets of their past, to Isaiah and to Amos, to Jeremiah and to Habakkuk.

Some would indeed respond, but, then as now, many would be blind and deaf to the Saviour of the world.

For further reflection and action

1. Jesus seemed to have a special concern for poor and marginalised people. Who are the poor and marginalised today, and how can we follow Jesus in reaching out to them?

2. In Romans 9—11, Paul deals at length with the status of the Jews who have rejected Christ. These are difficult and much-debated chapters, requiring careful study, but reading 9:1–5, 30–33 and 10:1–4 will give you a flavour of Paul's argument.

3. Do you have friends and family who are content with their view on life and are indignant at attempts to present the gospel to them? Try to find two or three Christians and pray regularly together for the Holy Spirit's work in those lives, and for wisdom and discernment in your approach.

32: Love

'Do not think that I have come to abolish the Law or the Prophets; I have not come to abolish them but to fulfil them.'
MATTHEW 5:17

'So in everything, do to others what you would have them do to you, for this sums up the Law and the Prophets.'
MATTHEW 7:12

One of them, an expert in the law, tested [Jesus] with this question: 'Teacher, which is the greatest commandment in the Law?' Jesus replied: '"Love the Lord your God with all your heart and with all your soul and with all your mind." This is the first and greatest commandment. And the second is like it: "Love your neighbour as yourself." All the Law and the Prophets hang on these two commandments.'
MATTHEW 22:35–40

Matthew 5—7, known as the Sermon on the Mount, sets out the way of life of those who belong to the kingdom. From beginning to end, it assumes a world that we know—where people hurt others through anger, where women are demeaned through lust, where marriages collapse, where Christians are persecuted, where we worry about what to eat and what to wear even while others are forced to beg. Sound familiar?

We live in this world, but we do so as Jesus' disciples, disciples of the one who, according to his own claim, fulfils the Law and the Prophets. Faithfulness to Jesus entails faithfulness to all that has gone before in God's dealings with his people through law-giver and prophet—but only as Jesus fulfils it. This means that the Sermon on the Mount is not just about getting to the 'true meaning' of the Law, but about knowing and following the one to whom the Law points. Far from setting aside the Law and the Prophets, Jesus carries them into a new era of fulfilment in which his authoritative voice will govern the disciples' obedience.

Matthew 7:12 reinforces what is apparent throughout the sermon—that our discipleship happens in relationship not just with God but with others. Jesus declares that doing to others what we would have them do to us is the Law and the Prophets (echoing 5:17), the true direction towards which the Old Testament points.

He makes the same point to the lawyer in Matthew 22:34–40, where the whole Law and the Prophets are said to 'hang on' love for God and neighbour. The Old Testament continues in full force for disciples of Christ, but—mediated through Jesus who fulfils it—its regulations are understood and embodied as expressions of love of God and of one's neighbour, worked out in every aspect of life.

All of this shows that Jesus' teaching is not concerned with constructing a system of disembodied rules but with reorientating the whole of life around a new reality—God's inbreaking reign. Jesus' exhortations are not faceless demands; rather, they presuppose certain things about him and about the kingdom he brings, which means that the Law and Prophets are no longer the centre of gravity—Jesus is. We are not just called to live a particular lifestyle but to follow a peerless Lord.

For further reflection and action

1. The principle emerging from Matthew 5:17–20 appears to be that all the Old Testament law applies to Christians, but none of it applies apart from its fulfilment in Christ; its validity continues only with reference to him. Look at the examples in Matthew 5:21–48 to see how this principle works out in practice.

2. Why might it be important not to abstract Jesus' demands from the story told in the gospel as a whole, which reaches its culmination in the death and resurrection?

3. For Paul, too, love is the fulfilment of the law (Romans 13:8–10; see also Galatians 5:13–15). Think and pray about your week ahead—at work and at home—and the opportunities you will have to express love for God and love for others.

33: Listen! Whoever has ears...

Then the disciples came to him and asked, 'Why do you speak to the people in parables?' He replied, 'Because the knowledge of the secrets of the kingdom of heaven has been given to you, but not to them... Blessed are your eyes because they see, and your ears because they hear.'

MATTHEW 13:10–11, 16

Jesus taught in parables—longish ones with characters and plot (such as the prodigal son), ones with detailed, sometimes allegorical, interpretations (the sower), and others expressed as short metaphors (the woman making bread with yeast). Sometimes we know the context. Jesus stood in a boat, Matthew tells us, to tell the story of the sower to a large crowd on the shore. Afterwards the disciples asked him what it meant and he explained it to them. More often, though, we are given no explanation.

Over the centuries, the parables have presented some knotty problems of interpretation. Did Jesus just make up stories, or was the sower, for example, to be seen on the hill above him, doing exactly what Jesus says? Is the story of the man paying the same wages, however long the labourers had worked, any guide for employers today? Is there just one main truth per parable or should we be teasing lessons out of every element in the story? Will we really be able to watch the damned from heaven, as in the story of the rich man and Lazarus?

Unlike the first three Gospel writers, John never uses the word 'parable', but his use of extended metaphors—light and darkness, sheep and shepherds, hunger and the bread of life, thirst and living water, the vine and the vine dresser—help us see that Jesus is building on images and metaphors used by the prophets and sages of the Old Testament.

Jesus' answer to the disciples' question in Matthew 13:11 gives us a clue, maybe even the key, to what is involved when he teaches in parables. The disciples are distinguished from the crowds not by their instant and intuitive understanding of Jesus' parables, but by their seeking of explanations, and by having the 'secrets' revealed to them. Inherent in every parable, short or long, is a question: Do you understand? Are your ears and eyes open to the truth?

Jesus draws a picture with which we can immediately engage, but which carries a truth that we may miss. A humble, passionate desire to know him and his will for us is the beginning of our understanding and appropriation of parable truth. In addition, those whose own eyes have been opened will want to alert others to the presence and power of the kingdom, inviting people to listen and respond when the king calls.

For further reflection and action

1. Ezekiel 34:1–24, God's promise to send a shepherd to tend the people of Israel, seems to lie behind a number of passages about shepherding and sheep in the Gospels. How, for instance, might it inform our understanding of what's going on in Luke 15:1–7?

2. Look at the parable of the good Samaritan in Luke 10: 25–37. The legal expert wants to know who qualifies as a neighbour whom he should love. Imagine that you are

leading a study of the parable and you ask the group this question ('Who is your neighbour?') before reading it. How do you think they would reply? In the telling of the story, what are the main points that Jesus is making about neighbour-love?

3. How far should Jesus' teaching in parables provide a model for communicating with people today? As you think about this, reflect on why the apostles in the book of Acts did not appear to use parables in their own preaching.

34: Powerful in deed

While they were eating, Jesus took bread, and when he had given thanks, he broke it and gave it to his disciples, saying, 'Take and eat; this is my body.' Then he took a cup, and when he had given thanks, he gave it to them, saying, 'Drink from it, all of you. This is my blood of the covenant, which is poured out for many for the forgiveness of sins. I tell you, I will not drink from this fruit of the vine from now on until that day when I drink it new with you in my Father's kingdom.'
MATTHEW 26:26–29

Sometimes, words alone didn't work, and the prophets themselves became living embodiments of God's message. Jeremiah, for instance, walked around Jerusalem with a wooden yoke on his neck (Jeremiah 27:2), calling on the people to submit to God. Jesus stands in this tradition of faithful prophets who not only spoke God's word but also performed symbol-laden actions in order to make a point.

Thus it is that Jesus' act of gathering twelve disciples can be seen as a symbol of gathering the twelve tribes of Israel to be a renewed people of God. Thus it is that his eating and drinking with society's outcasts effectively redraws the boundaries of holiness and redefines who is acceptable to dine in God's kingdom.

Many of Jesus' significant symbolic acts are clustered in the final week of his ministry. According to Matthew 21, he enters Jerusalem in deliberate fulfilment of a messianic prophecy (Zechariah 9:9–10). The hopes of the prophets (and of the people on the Jerusalem streets, singing Psalm 118:25–26) were that God would one day establish a son of David on the throne in Jerusalem and restore the fortunes of the people. That day is now dawning—except that Jesus chooses to ride on a beast of burden rather than a war-horse. What follows is Jesus' action in the temple, the place to which God's 'messenger of the covenant' would come (Malachi 3:1–5). Whether this dramatic incident should be understood as a cleansing of the temple from its abuses, to restore it as a place of prayer for Jew and non-Jew alike, or whether it should be seen as symbolic of God's forthcoming judgment on the temple, Jesus' action issues a challenge to the religious authorities, which sets in motion the controversies of the final week leading to his arrest and trial.

Then, stepping aside with his disciples—as he breaks bread and pours wine—he reshapes the Passover meal around his own forthcoming death, which will bring about a new release from bondage. More than this, the new covenant between God and his people includes the forward-looking promise of eating and drinking again in the future kingdom. But it is Jesus' death that makes possible the future feast for which we hope.

Jesus' actions challenge us to reflect on the true meaning

of his kingship: power and glory, yes, but in humility and obedience. And he encourages us, as he encouraged the disciples, to model our lives after the pattern of his death, that we might love him and serve each other.

For further reflection and action

1. What practical steps can we take to invite outcasts into the community of the church? Think about those times when you have been grateful for someone else's hospitality, and consider who you might show hospitality to, even by an act as simple as inviting someone for a meal.

2. Read John 13:1–17 and reflect on Jesus' washing of the disciples' feet as another symbolic action. What, according to John's account, does the act symbolise and what is its significance for followers of Christ?

3. We are not Jesus or Jeremiah, of course, but in what ways might we be personal embodiments of God's message to people today?

35: Finished!

Later, knowing that everything had now been finished, and so that Scripture would be fulfilled, Jesus said, 'I am thirsty.' A jar of wine vinegar was there, so they soaked a sponge in it, put the sponge on a stalk of the hyssop plant, and lifted it to Jesus' lips. When he had received the drink, Jesus said, 'It is finished.' With that, he bowed his head and gave up his spirit.
JOHN 19:28–30

For God was pleased to have all his fullness dwell in him, and through him to reconcile to himself all things, whether things on earth or things in heaven, by making peace through his blood, shed on the cross.

COLOSSIANS 1:19–20

We anticipate the dawn of a new day in the resurrection, but, for the moment at least, we pause at Good Friday—and pause we must, for the biblical story makes no sense without the events of this day. As we pause, we join with Christians around the globe and through the ages who have confessed the centrality of Christ's work on the cross, for our faith makes no sense without it.

The cross, of course, is where the Gospels—and Jesus—have been heading since the start. As he dies, he takes on the role of the servant spoken of in Isaiah 53, suffering and dying on behalf of others. The fact that it happens at Passover time gives his death an 'exodus' flavour, as Jesus brings about a new release for the people of God, inaugurating a new covenant in his body and blood for the forgiveness of sins.

The predicament of human beings, so apparent in the biblical story—our rebellion against God and the judgment it deserves—is dealt with at the cross, interpreted in the early church as a demonstration of God's love and as a victory over the powers of darkness. This sacrifice of one in the place of others is what makes forgiveness possible, bringing about reconciliation with God and with each other, and more besides.

The work of the cross is applied personally, though not privately, for it is the place where the wisdom and power of God are demonstrated to the world. Paul makes clear the comprehensive nature of what has been accomplished—not just on our behalf but on behalf of the whole of creation. Jesus' death is God's chosen means of restoring 'all things', liberating men and women, and creation itself, from sin and bondage, with the guarantee that one day evil will be removed completely.

So the cross stands not just at the peak of the Gospels but at the climax of the entire history of salvation. Everything in the biblical story leads up to and away from this point; everything is understood in the light it casts, a light extending forward to the final victory when all things will be fully restored.

Meanwhile, that light illumines our discipleship and mission as we seek to make sense of the cross and be shaped by it, knowing that we live by faith in the Son of God who loved us and gave himself for us.

For further reflection and action

1. All four Gospels devote considerable space to the death of Jesus and the events leading up to it. As Martin Kahler famously observed, they can be seen as 'passion narratives with extended introductions'.[6] Reflect on how far you agree with this as a good description of the Gospels.

2. The pattern of the cross and resurrection is one of suffering followed by glory. If Christian discipleship involves a call to follow the way of the cross, think of the moments in your life or the lives of others where this pattern has been evident.

3. How does the cross transform the ordinary stuff of life (the 'all things' of Colossians 1), and how do we follow the way of the cross in that ordinary stuff?

36: Alleluia! He is risen!

Early on the first day of the week, while it was still dark, Mary Magdalene went to the tomb and saw that the stone had been removed from the entrance… On the evening of that first day of the week, when the disciples were together, with the doors locked for fear of the Jewish leaders, Jesus came and stood among them and said, 'Peace be with you!' After he said this, he showed them his hands and side. The disciples were overjoyed when they saw the Lord.

JOHN 20:1, 19–20

A new day, a new dawn—a new creation. Just as the first infinitesimal part of a second at the beginning of the universe was a unique and unrepeated moment, so the resurrection of Jesus—Saviour, Lord and God—was the first, unique, unprecedented, unparalleled moment when God's promised new creation began. Without the resurrection, the cross is a defeat; there is no forgiveness, no salvation, no new life and no hope beyond death. But thanks be to God! He gives us the victory over death through our Lord Jesus Christ.

We know that our declaration of faith, 'I believe in the resurrection of the body', will be fulfilled for us who are his, when he comes again in glory and the new heaven and the new earth are fully realised. As Tom Wright puts it, 'With Jesus of Nazareth there is not simply a new religious possibility, not simply a new ethic or a new way of salvation, but a new creation.'[7]

It took some time for the amazing truth of the resurrection, with all its stunning implications, to dawn on the disciples. We see a progression from their disbelief when the women came back from the tomb and told them it was so, to Peter's Spirit-filled sermon at Pentecost and Paul's dramatic words to the Colossians: 'He is the beginning and the firstborn from among the dead, so that in everything he might have the supremacy. For God was pleased to have all his fullness dwell in him' (1:18–19).

Meanwhile, what are the implications for everyday life?

Again, Tom Wright is helpful:

Because the early Christians believed that 'resurrection' had begun with Jesus, and would be completed in the great final resurrection on the last day, they believed that God had called them to work with him, in the power of the Spirit, to implement the achievement of Jesus and thereby to anticipate the final resurrection, in personal and political life, in mission and holiness.[8]

Those who belong to Jesus are called to whole-life discipleship, to the resurrection life of the kingdom, whereby in every corner of our lives we are charged with transforming the present, as far as we were able, in the light of that future.

For further reflection and action

1. If you are part of a home group or prayer group, it might be interesting and helpful to ask each other these questions. How do we think Jesus' resurrection relates to our own survival after death? Will we have resurrection bodies or will we survive as 'souls' freed from physical form? Tom Wright's book, *Surprised by Hope*, offers a helpful treatment of these questions.

2. Isaiah 38:9–20 records Hezekiah's poem about being close to death. Compare his sentiments with Paul's teaching in 1 Corinthians 15.

3. Can you think of times in your life when you have brought resurrection life into your daily activities? Some may point to running an allotment, teaching a child to read, sitting with a friend in hospital, encouraging a colleague at work, or giving money to good causes. How would it change our days if we woke each morning reminding ourselves that we are agents of God's resurrection transformation?

37: The great project

Jesus came to them and said, 'All authority in heaven and on earth has been given to me. Therefore go and make disciples of all nations, baptising them in the name of the Father and of the Son and of the Holy Spirit, and teaching them to obey everything I have commanded you. And surely I am with you always, to the very end of the age.'

MATTHEW 28:18–20

With a world-changing chapter, Matthew rounds off his Gospel. Jesus bursts from death to life, and the disciples are commissioned to turn the world upside down.

In a sense, this was a briefing for the work that was to follow the outpouring of the Holy Spirit, which empowered the church for its mission. It was a briefing that told them what their mission was to be, but it also tells us what our mission is to be. The all-important directive—to 'make disciples'— is sandwiched between the affirmation of Jesus' authority and the promise of his presence. Entitled and enabled by his authority (v. 18), and supported and strengthened by his presence (v. 20), his people are sent into the world.

Indeed, it is to the whole world that they are sent—to all nations, not only to the Jews but also to the Gentiles—reminding us once again of the global dimension of the biblical story, from the creation of the world in Genesis to the promise in Revelation that all nations will walk in the light of the Lamb of God.

Interestingly, 'make disciples' is the main command in these verses. Of course, the 'making disciples' assumes a 'going', but all of us go in this sense, whatever we are doing. We go about our everyday life with new values and a new sense of purpose; we follow the Lord's call to the ends of the earth; we make disciples. And integral to the process of making disciples is both baptising them (as a way of enabling them to say who they belong to—God, Father, Son, and Holy Spirit) and teaching them everything Jesus has commanded: to be not just hearers or learners, but doers of his word.

Jesus commissioned his disciples, and he commissions all Christians ever since, to make disciples—people who submit to the authority of the master, people who not only understand the teaching of the master but also obey it, people who are committed to living the way the master calls them to live in all areas of their lives. 'Disciples making other disciples' is at the heart of the church's mission. It's a commission that puts disciple-making as the main agenda and top priority of every Christian, of every church.

This, then, is our mission—to be whole-life disciples who make whole-life disciples.

Will we embrace it?

For further reflection and action

1. I need to do a health check on my own life. Am I truly a whole-life disciple or are there areas of my life that I am reluctant to surrender to Christ's Lordship?

2. As we make big plans for the future—for example, changing jobs or moving house—how, if at all, should the 'great commission' influence our decisions?

3. Are there Christian friends or members of your church whom you might more intentionally seek to disciple? If you feel that you need someone to mentor you, can you identify someone you might approach? What is it that makes them 'fit for purpose'?

38: Out of this world?

When he had led them out to the vicinity of Bethany, he lifted up his hands and blessed them. While he was blessing them, he left them and was taken up into heaven. Then they worshipped him and returned to Jerusalem with great joy. And they stayed continually at the temple, praising God.

LUKE 24:50–53

Christ's ascension sometimes gets bundled together with his resurrection rather than being treated as an event in its own right. In fact, as the rhythm of the church's calendar reminds us, the two events were separated by 40 days. That rhythm, itself informed by the biblical story, enables us to see things as they really are—from God's perspective—with Jesus' ascension opening up a new era in the history of his dealings with the world and his people in the world.

At the very least, it means that Jesus is exalted to the right hand of God, as Peter explains (Acts 2:33–36; 5:31), showing that he is less interested in the 'up–down' mechanics of the event than he is with the status of his Lord. The ascension confirms Jesus as the king, the fulfilment of God's promises to David.

Beyond this, if we lose the ascension, we lose the heavenly ministry of Jesus as our high priest, his very presence with God providing intercession on our behalf, his finished work requiring no repetition or extension of any kind. Lose the ascension and we risk losing the comfort of hope—that one day our weak bodies will be like his glorious body, that the same Jesus who ascended will return as judge and king. And he will return as a man too—for he did not slip off his humanity to get on with the task of being the exalted Son of God, but has taken it into the very presence of God, wedding us to him for ever, reminding us once again of God's commitment to restore his creation.

The ascension does not mark the end of Jesus' work on earth but the continuation of it through the church. Our mission can be carried out with confidence because of the position our master now occupies, with all places subject to his rule and all people subject to his oversight, including the places we inhabit and the people we encounter, even today.

As the ascended Lord, he lays claim not just to the church but to all realms of life; and his heavenly location redraws the way we think about our 'location'—how we live in our earthly 'spaces', given the one from whom we take our bearing. Our lives are oriented around the reality of the risen and ascended

Christ, his heavenly Lordship investing today's apparently menial tasks with eternal significance.

For further reflection and action

1. An old adage suggests that some Christians can be too heavenly-minded to be of any earthly use. In keeping with our reflections on Christ's ascension, how far is it important for us to be heavenly-minded precisely so that we can be of earthly use (see Colossians 3:1)?

2. Read and reflect on some of the passages in Hebrews that describe Jesus' ascension and ministry as the great high priest: 1:3; 2:9; 4:14–16; 6:19–20; 7:23—8:2; 10:19–25; 12:2.

3. Try to chat with a fellow Christian this week about the ongoing significance of the ascension for our lives as disciples of Christ.

Church

39: A new world order?

When the day of Pentecost came, they were all together in one place. Suddenly a sound like the blowing of a violent wind came from heaven and filled the whole house where they were sitting. They saw what seemed to be tongues of fire that separated and came to rest on each of them. All of them were filled with the Holy Spirit and began to speak in other tongues as the Spirit enabled them. Now there were staying in Jerusalem God-fearing Jews from every nation under heaven... Utterly amazed, they asked: 'Aren't all these who are speaking Galileans? Then how is it that each of us hears them in our native language? ... We hear them declaring the wonders of God in our own tongues!'

ACTS 2:1–5, 7–8, 11

Pentecost was a harvest festival, an opportunity for thankful worshippers to offer to God the firstfruits of their crops. Celebrated 50 days after Passover, coinciding with the anniversary of the giving of the law, it also became associated with the covenant made between the Lord and his people at Sinai. The nation that was constituted at Sinai, gathering together in Jerusalem to renew their relationship with God, is now, so many years later, reborn—the firstfruits of a new harvest, as God pours out his Spirit to ratify the new covenant.

Certainly, Peter is aware that something momentous has

happened. His subsequent explanation makes this clear as he ties together the ministry, death, resurrection and exaltation of Jesus with several passages from scripture, notably God's promise through Joel that 'I will pour out my Spirit on all people' (Joel 2:28). Previously the Spirit was given only to special people, such as kings and prophets, or only for specific tasks; now all of God's people receive the Spirit—men and women, old and young—as part of God's end-time renewal of all things. Pentecost marks the beginning of that era, not with Moses giving the law, but with Jesus giving the Spirit to 'everyone who calls on the name of the Lord' (Acts 2:21).

In fact, this is nothing less than the inauguration of a new world. It may remind us of the story of Babel (Genesis 11:1–9), but it is not necessarily a reversal of Babel—where the scattering reaffirmed God's original purpose for men and women to fill the whole earth. The basis of the unity of humankind is found not in the recovery of a single language but in a people indwelt by the Spirit of God. If there is a reversal, it is that, at Babel, people wanted to make a name for themselves (v. 4), whereas at Pentecost they proclaim 'the wonders of God'. Many languages are spoken, and all are appropriate for giving praise to God.

This fits with the international perspective of Acts. Jerusalem is full of Jews from every part of the known world, each with their own language and dialect. They hear the great deeds of God spoken of in the vernacular tongues of their pagan neighbours—showing that what starts in Jerusalem will become a worldwide mission enabled by the Holy Spirit, which will result in the worship of God to 'the ends of the earth' (Acts 1:8).

For further reflection and action

1. Read the whole of Acts 2, reflecting on Peter's explanation of the event (vv. 14–41) and its immediate impact on the early followers of Christ (vv. 42–47).

2. Many Christians belong to a Pentecostal denomination, but in what sense—and with what significance—are all God's people 'Pentecostals'?

3. We might be used to the notion of the priesthood of all believers, but Acts 2 suggests there is also a prophethood of all believers (vv. 17–21). Previously the Holy Spirit had enabled mainly prophets to speak God's words (see Numbers 11:29); now, speaking the word of God—prophesying—is a task given to all of God's people (Acts 4:31; 5:32; 6:10; 13:4–5). How should this encourage us? And how should it challenge us?

40: Acts of God

Now those who had been scattered by the persecution that broke out when Stephen was killed travelled as far as Phoenicia, Cyprus and Antioch, spreading the word only among Jews. Some of them, however, men from Cyprus and Cyrene, went to Antioch and began to speak to Greeks also, telling them the good news about the Lord Jesus. The Lord's hand was with them, and a great number of people believed and turned to the Lord... The disciples were called Christians first at Antioch.

ACTS 11:19–21, 26

Luke makes it clear that the account he tells in Acts is a continuation of the story he began in his Gospel (Acts 1:1–2). In fact, it is the next phase of the story that goes back to God's promise to Abraham and the vocation of Israel to be a light to the nations. That calling, embodied supremely in Jesus, is now passed on to his followers as they continue God's mission, bearing witness—across cultural, ethnic and geographical boundaries—that his salvation will extend to 'the ends of the earth' (Acts 1:8).

The biggest personality in this phase of the story, of course, is Paul, who makes three separate journeys, travelling through the Roman Empire, proclaiming Jesus, establishing churches and returning to instruct them or writing to them.

It is equally apparent, though, that the work was carried out by 'ordinary' believers, who spread the word wherever they went (8:4). We don't know the names of those who established the church in Antioch, but we do know that it was this multicultural mix of Jewish and Gentile believers who were first given the designation 'Christian'. And it was this church that became the base for sending out others (Barnabas and Paul, no less, 13:1–3), launching a mission into the wider Roman world. Rightly the church carries out God's work in its own place, and rightly it keeps in mind that the gospel is for all nations.

Beyond numerical growth, it's also apparent that the work of the Spirit is embodied in the lives of the new communities formed—in prayer and worship, in distinct patterns of life together, in following the apostles' teaching and in economic practices. This means that the church is not just one more social organisation within Roman society, but a community that, by its very nature, witnesses to the presence of God's kingdom. Faith, then, is not merely private or interior but lived out on the public stage, engaged in the world.

Throughout, the centre of gravity is God himself: mission is not what the church does, but what God does through the church. The same gracious God, the same exalted Christ, the same powerful Spirit and the same amazing plan mean that we too play a part in the continual unfolding of this story, witnessing to a renewed relationship with God and the restoration of the whole of life under the Lordship of Christ.

For further reflection and action

1. How would you describe the influence and role played by the book of Acts in (a) your own life as a Christian, and (b) the life and ministry of the church to which you belong?

2. Read some passages in Acts (for example, 2:42–47; 11:19–21; 13:1–3) that describe the early Christian communities. What are the recurring characteristics, and what picture of the church is built up from passages like these?

3. What might be some of the problems with using the book of Acts as a blueprint for churches today? How do we decide what applies and does not apply in our own time and place?

41: No Spirit, no Church

There are different kinds of gifts, but the same Spirit. There are different kinds of service, but the same Lord. There are different kinds of working, but in all of them and in everyone it is the same God at work.

1 CORINTHIANS 12:4–6

The pouring out of the Holy Spirit at Pentecost introduced a new element into the lives of the believers. Until that point, their identity and unity had been based on their personal knowledge of Jesus, or on the faith engendered by accounts of his resurrection. Then came the overwhelming experience in Jerusalem, heralded by the appearance of fire and the sound of a mighty wind. As we come to this stage in the biblical account, then, we find ourselves in the drama of God's dealings with us, his people—indwelt by the Spirit, joined together in the body of Christ.

As the early group of believers evolved into the church, the Spirit was an acknowledged presence. So, Paul writes to the Ephesians about the church as a building, a 'dwelling in which God lives by his Spirit' (2:22), bound together in 'the unity of the Spirit' (4:3); and, to the Romans, of the experiential love that God pours into our hearts 'through the Holy Spirit, who has been given to us' (5:5).

Essentially, the Spirit initiates people into the church and empowers them once they are in. Gordon D. Fee, commenting on 1 Corinthians 12:13, writes, 'Such expressive metaphors (immersion in the Spirit and drinking to the fill of the Spirit)... do imply a much greater experiential and visibly manifest reception of the Spirit than many have tended to experience in subsequent church history.'[9] That the experience of the Spirit is not discussed much in Paul's letters (except in 1 Corinthians, where it seems to have been confusing and divisive) is no proof that it was unimportant. Indeed, it is highly likely that Paul took that experience for granted as part of the full 'package' of salvation.

Clearly the Corinthians were confused by the *charismata*, the 'gifts of the Spirit', and, being a church riven by division, were misusing these gifts, particularly those that were seen to be more spectacular. But Paul's main point is to emphasise the great variety of spiritual gifts, and that they are the work of God for the upbuilding of the church.

Few of us would deny the need for the manifest presence and power of God in our sceptical and rationalistic age. Differences in our personalities and in our callings will require different gifts, which God gives to each of us according to his will. In line with Paul's exhortations, let us never be guilty of quenching the Spirit (1 Thessalonians 5:19); rather, may we 'eagerly desire gifts of the Spirit' (1 Corinthians 14:1).

For further reflection and action

1. In addition to looking more widely at Paul's discussion in 1 Corinthians 12—14, read and reflect on other passages that deal with gifts given for the overall good of the body of Christ: Romans 12:3–8 and Ephesians 4:1–16.

2. How far does our self-reliance, our rationalism or our fear of ridicule hinder us from seeking the fullness of the Spirit in our lives or in our churches?

3. Do we allow ourselves to be challenged by stories of miraculous healing or provision? Are we brave enough eagerly to desire, and to use, whatever gift the Lord may want to give us?

42: The freedom of the Spirit

It is for freedom that Christ has set us free. Stand firm, then, and do not let yourselves be burdened again by a yoke of slavery... So I say, walk by the Spirit, and you will not gratify the desires of the flesh... But the fruit of the Spirit is love, joy, peace, forbearance, kindness, goodness, faithfulness, gentleness and self-control... Since we live by the Spirit, let us keep in step with the Spirit.

GALATIANS 5:1, 16, 22–23, 25

Guilty and condemned, awaiting sentence, the prisoner hears the judge say, 'It is for freedom that Christ has set you free.' Reconciled to God through the cross, we are free—free from the law, free from the power of sin, free from the fear of death, free to live and serve the Lord who has freed us, in the power of his Spirit.

Free, but not perfect! The Holy Spirit has made us new creations, already enjoying our inheritance in the new Jerusalem, already signed-up citizens of the kingdom of God; but the 'sinful nature', or 'flesh', is not completely vanquished and the world around us is still troubled and sometimes very dark.

So we live by the Spirit in this world between the ages, until, at last, we and all the saints will reign with God in the new creation. At our conversion, God begins through the Spirit to exercise his claim on every aspect of our lives. Here in Galatians, Paul outlines some of the ways the Spirit works in the individual believer.

Our freedom, our new life in Christ, is a free gift of grace— 'not of ourselves' in any way (compare Ephesians 2:8–9). But then Paul calls us to 'keep in step', to run the race, to be transformed. This is a calling to a lifelong cooperation with the Spirit's work, transforming our personalities, growing the fruit of the Spirit and changing us into the likeness of Christ. But it's not automatic: we can hinder the Spirit's work in our lives and in our communities.

Beyond producing his fruit in us, the Spirit works through other people and through all the influences and experiences of life, in ordinary ways and, sometimes, in extraordinary ways—such as dreams, words of knowledge, discernment and wisdom for particular situations (1 Corinthians 12:4– 13). He also works to bring the word of God alive to us (John 14:25–26), renewing our minds (Romans 12:2) so that we are better able to bring the transforming power of his love into the everyday worlds we inhabit.

For further reflection and action

1. 'Do not quench the Spirit. Do not treat prophecies with contempt, but test them all,' says Paul in 1 Thessalonians 5:19–21. Looking back, are you aware of times when you have quenched the Spirit in some way? Have you ever failed to test an action or a change of course that seemed to be right at the time?

2. The fruit of the Spirit listed in Galatians 5 are not, of course, the only virtues that Christians are encouraged to develop under the Holy Spirit's leading. Paul and the other Bible writers mention others. Some people have commented that they might be characterised as more feminine than masculine virtues! Where are courage, decisiveness, strength and discipline? Where are our society's current favourite virtues—such as flexibility, tolerance, celebrity and humour? (This could make an interesting discussion!)

3. In the process of assessing ourselves and repenting of our lack of love, joy and so on, how much does it help to have one or two very close friends who can pray with us and assist us in our cooperation with the Spirit?

43: How RU CU L8R Love Paul

It is no trouble for me to write the same things to you again, and it is a safeguard for you.

PHILIPPIANS 3:1

No Royal Mail, no telephones, no email, no text messaging. How were the apostles to communicate with the numerous churches that sprang up in the years after Jesus' resurrection?

The New Testament letters are a priceless resource for us, 2000 years later, containing the bulk of the doctrinal and ethical teaching that has defined the Christian life and informed the church through the ages. But what were these letters to their original recipients? If not their lifeblood (that, surely, was the Spirit himself), then they were their sustenance, their diet, their nutrition.

The letters give us astonishing insight into the life of these early churches and a unique body of teaching. Writing to the Romans, Paul establishes the essential principle of justification by faith in Christ (3:21—5:1). To the Galatians, who were being pressed to observe the Jewish law in addition to their faith (2:11—3:25), he becomes passionate and forthright: 'Are you so foolish? After beginning by means of the Spirit, are you now trying to finish by means of the flesh?' (3:3). James, for his part, recognising that some Christians were beginning to presume too much on their faith, argues that genuine faith has to express itself in action: 'Faith by itself, if it is not accompanied by action, is dead' (2:17).

All the writers ground their moral and ethical exhortations on the great truths of God's salvation in Christ—even though the letters differ in style and in the situations that they address. For instance, while Paul's letters to the Galatians and the Colossians seek to correct false teaching from outside the church, others, particularly the Corinthian correspondence, highlight problems and dilemmas that were causing trouble within the church.

Paul's approach to these particular issues establishes broader principles, which can be seen to be applicable in our own day. 'Do you not know that your bodies are members of Christ himself?' he demands. 'Shall I then take the members of Christ and unite them with a prostitute? Never!' (1 Corinthians 6:15). Other examples include the Corinthians' question about eating food sacrificed to idols (8:4–13). Again, he tells them, 'You are the body of Christ' (12:27), and on this fact he builds his teaching about the church.

Above all else, however, the New Testament letters interpret Christ, revealing him in his glory and his sacrificial love, and giving hope to his people in every age.

For further reflection and action

1. Reflect on the significance of the fact that the New Testament contains several letters addressed to the particular situations and needs of different churches. How might this help in our application of them to today's world?

2. How far are we willing to subject our own churches and denominations to the probing light of the letters? Do we personally allow ourselves to be challenged, in our thinking and behaviour, by the truths they expound?

3. Can we seek, in our generation, to revive or maintain the art of letter-writing, to bring truth, encouragement and hope to others? How might we do so? How do email, Facebook, Twitter and other forms of social media work in this respect?

44: Elect and scattered

Peter, an apostle of Jesus Christ, to God's elect, exiles scattered throughout the provinces... You are a chosen people, a royal priesthood, a holy nation, God's special possession, that you may declare the praises of him who called you out of darkness into his wonderful light. Once you were not a people, but now you are the people of God; once you had not received mercy, but now you have received mercy.

1 PETER 1:1; 2:9–10

The LORD called to [Moses] from the mountain and said...
'Although the whole earth is mine, you will be for me a kingdom of priests and a holy nation.'

EXODUS 19:3, 5–6 (ABRIDGED)

Peter wrote to the churches of Asia Minor, small fellowships
of Jews and Gentiles, and gave them a new and powerful
identity, using the titles given by God to the newly formed
nation of Israel at Sinai.

As we read the New Testament documents, we can see
how the writers were being led by the Holy Spirit into a new
understanding of what it means to be God's people. The
life, death, resurrection and ascension of Jesus had taken
them into a new age. Now Jew and Gentile together were
the church, the redeemed people of God. But this did not
mean simply that Gentiles should become Jews, grafted in
to all that Judaism entailed—law and regulations for living,
temple and sacrifices, land and ethnic identity. Nor did it
mean, however, that these elements were swept away and
forgotten as a new faith sprang into life.

Now, all the great symbolic identity markers of Israel are
pulled into focus, finding their final significance through
the cross and resurrection of Jesus Christ. He is our sacrifice
(Hebrews 9:11–14); his body is the temple destroyed and
rebuilt in three days (John 2:19). Now we, as Christians, are
also identified as temples of the Holy Spirit, both individually
and together (2 Corinthians 6:16; Ephesians 2:21). Now there
is no longer one ethnic group in one geographically outlined
land, but new communities of 'persons from every tribe and
language and people and nation', who have been made 'to be
a kingdom and priests to serve our God' (Revelation 5:9–10).
The whole heritage of Israel, from Abraham through David to

John the Baptist, has been transformed into the heritage of his redeemed and chosen people throughout the earth.

The emphasis falls on continuity and fulfilment. Peter, like other New Testament writers, believes that Jesus is Israel's Messiah and hopes that all Jews will now gather around that Messiah, but he is also aware that God is finally fulfilling his promise to bring the Gentiles into the blessing too.

That blessing gives them the privileges and responsibilities that went with the covenant. Hence, Israel's call—its identity and role with respect to the world—is now taken up by the church, by every follower of Christ. God's mission to bless all nations continues to be worked out through us, his chosen people—wherever we may find ourselves 'scattered'—placed in the world for the sake of the world.

For further reflection and action

1. Many Christians believe that the promises of God to Israel have now come to their final fruition in Christ and in the people of God composed of Jews and Gentiles together in one body. Other Christians believe that God still has a special plan for Israel and that (for instance) the return of Jews to Palestine in the 20th century was part of that plan. Which view do you hold, and why?

2. If there are no chosen nations, no ethnicities special to God, and perhaps no land with a particular and unique blessing, but all barriers are broken down and Christians are all one in Christ, what are the implications for our churches? What are the divisions that still affect our lives together?

3. In his book *The Radical Disciple* (IVP, 2010), John Stott writes, 'I doubt if there is any New Testament text which gives a more varied and balanced account of what it means to be a disciple than 1 Peter 2:1–17.' Read the passage and reflect on his assessment of its 'varied and balanced account'.

45: Living between the times

I consider that our present sufferings are not worth comparing with the glory that will be revealed in us... The creation itself will be liberated from its bondage to decay and brought into the freedom and glory of the children of God. We know that the whole creation has been groaning as in the pains of childbirth right up to the present time. Not only so, but we ourselves, who have the firstfruits of the Spirit, groan inwardly as we wait eagerly for our adoption to sonship, the redemption of our bodies. For in this hope we were saved.

ROMANS 8:18, 21–24

This passage is one of many in which Paul expresses the tension between how things are now and how they will be one day. That tension, which is part and parcel of everyday discipleship, is bound up with the biblical storyline—that which is promised under the old covenant receives a measure of fulfilment in Jesus and the church, but still awaits future consummation.

Jesus announces the arrival and presence of God's reign in his ministry and demonstrates its power in mighty works that bring restoration and renewal. Yet he also calls on his disciples to pray, 'Your kingdom come' (Matthew 6:10) and to watch and wait for the complete exercise of God's rule in the future. Rightly it has been said that we live in the period between the decisive battle and the definitive victory.

For Paul, too, there is an 'already' and a 'not yet' aspect to Christian experience. The new age has broken into the present age, so that we enjoy 'the firstfruits of the Spirit' while awaiting the full harvest. Indeed, the current experience of birth pains will give way to eventual relief. Perhaps reminiscent of the portrayal in Exodus 2:23–24 of the Israelites 'groaning' under their Egyptian slavery, Paul depicts salvation as a release from bondage, applying the imagery not just to men and women but to the entire created order. This is yet one more reminder of the comprehensive scope of God's work in Christ, where such liberation is not simply 'internal' or 'spiritual', but the 'redemption of our bodies' and of creation itself.

In this time between the times, we are called to witness to the ends of the earth. That mission—in keeping with what will be—is all-embracing, as we make known God's rule over the whole of life, announcing it with our lips as well as embodying it in our lives. Seeking to avoid both defeatism (claiming too little) and triumphalism (claiming too much), we can testify to the wide-ranging sweep of God's renewing power in politics and parenting, in economics and education, in art and athletics—being realistic about current 'bondage' but all the while looking forward to the complete restoration of what was originally declared 'good'.

Such is our confidence and expectation—our *hope*—a hope of the full disclosure of God's reign that shapes each of us in the here and now.

For further reflection and action

1. In line with the reference to 'the firstfruits of the Spirit' in Romans 8:23, reflect further on Ephesians 1:13–14 and 2 Corinthians 5:5, where Paul calls the Spirit a 'deposit' that guarantees our future inheritance. In what ways is our present experience of the Spirit a foretaste of the future?

2. If you're able to do so, pause every so often through the day to think about how the tension between the 'already' and the 'not yet' works itself out in your daily life.

3. To the Corinthians who think they have everything now, Paul emphasises that complete salvation lies in the future, at the resurrection—because he wants to downplay their triumphalism. In Colossians and Ephesians, on the other hand, he emphasises the present salvation we enjoy— already seated with Christ in heavenly places. What are the dangers in thinking that we have received everything now? What are the dangers of downplaying what we have already received? Which end of the tension do you gravitate towards, and why? As a particular case, what does the tension between the 'now' and the 'not yet' have to teach us about our hopes and expectations for healing?

*

Consummation

46: A forward-looking faith

We believe that Jesus died and rose again, and so we believe
that God will bring with Jesus those who have fallen asleep in
him… For the Lord himself will come down from heaven, with
a loud command, with the voice of the archangel and with
the trumpet call of God, and the dead in Christ will rise first.
After that, we who are still alive and are left will be caught up
together with them in the clouds to meet the Lord in the air.
And so we will be with the Lord for ever. Therefore encourage
one another with these words.

1 THESSALONIANS 4:14, 16–18

Paul looks back at what has gone before in the story of
redemption ('We believe that Jesus died and rose again') and
looks forward to what is to come ('and so we believe that
God will bring with Jesus those who have fallen asleep in
him'). One day, Jesus will be personally present as Lord of
the nations, king and judge, in a transformed and recreated
earth and heaven, the culmination of God's purposes for his
people and his world.

Jesus spoke about events to come in terms first used by
the Old Testament prophets, who themselves looked forward
to 'the day of the Lord'. Immediately after his ascension, the
apostles were told, 'This same Jesus, who has been taken
from you into heaven, will come back in the same way' (Acts
1:11). Now Paul, in the first letter to the Thessalonians,

dealing with their concerns about those who have already died, reassures them that the 'already dead' and the 'still alive' will rise and meet Jesus when he comes.

Of course, the rich metaphors and allusive language used to describe the return of Jesus can be confusing. A loud command, the archangel's call, the sound of the trumpet, Jesus coming in the clouds from heaven—all these word pictures are, in a sense, attempting to describe the unimaginable. They highlight the importance of humility when it comes to trying to describe exactly what will happen and when. Even so, it seems likely that when Paul talks about Jesus coming down and being met by a movement upwards, he is using words that describe a royal visit to a city, when a welcome party would be sent out to meet the prestigious visitor, returning with joy to the city. That's the image here, which implies that once our reunion has taken place, we will come back to the earth. And so, Paul says, 'we will be with the Lord for ever'.

Small wonder, then, that he calls on us to 'encourage one another with these words'. Like the Thessalonians, we will grieve the loss of loved ones and the separation that death brings, but we have a sure and certain hope. We will all be together at last, for he will come again to judge the living and the dead. Jesus will be personally present—the centre and focus of the new heaven and earth. He will reign and we will reign with him.

For further reflection and action

1. If you think about the second coming, how do you pict-ure it? Have you any expectations of the events that will precede it and those that will follow, after Jesus has

returned? Do you know why you hold these views on the way this present age will end?

2. Read a few other passages related to the return of Jesus: 2 Thessalonians 2:1–12; 2 Peter 3:10–13; Matthew 24: 29–44; Revelation 21:1–22:5. Rejoice in the sure and certain hope of Christ's coming.

3. Many Christians pay only lip service to Christ's return, in practice living as if the world will continue for ever as it is now. What difference would the perspective of eternity make to the way we might think about (a) material possessions, (b) other people, and (c) suffering?

47: Soul or body?

The body that is sown is perishable, it is raised imperishable; it is sown in dishonour, it is raised in glory; it is sown in weakness, it is raised in power; it is sown a natural body, it is raised a spiritual body.

1 CORINTHIANS 15:42–44

One of the major dimensions of the end of all things is the final resurrection. Indeed, the phrase from the Apostles' Creed, 'I believe in the resurrection of the body', reminds us that the goal of our salvation is not an immortal, immaterial soul but a glorious body.

Confusion surrounding the concept of 'eternal life' arguably goes right back to the culture prevalent at the time of the early church. It is commonly thought that Christians believe in the 'immortality of the soul'. But this was a Greek concept, put forward by (among others) Plato in his Dialogue *Phaedo*, in which he contrasts the pre-existent immortal soul with the corruptible human body. It is possible that Hellenistic converts to Christianity held this dualistic belief but Paul does not accept it. 'The perishable,' he wrote, 'must *clothe itself with* (or *put on*) the imperishable, and the mortal with immortality' (1 Corinthians 15:53).

As long as we think of an immaterial, spiritual 'heaven', we're likely to find it difficult to conceive of what Tom Wright, in his masterly book *Surprised by Hope*, describes as 'a new mode of physicality'.[10] But if, along with the apostle Paul, we conceive of Christ's return as inaugurating not only a new heaven but also a new earth, this physicality makes perfectly good sense. Wright suggests that the contrasting adjectives in 1 Corinthians 15:44 are misleadingly translated as 'natural' or 'physical', and 'spiritual'. Rather, he says, the contrast is between the present body, which is 'animated' by the human soul, and the future body, which is animated by the Spirit, 'God's breath of new life'.[11]

This way of understanding, astonishingly, liberates us from two of our great dilemmas about the future life: first, 'Shall we be able to recognise each other?' and second, 'Will all my present physical characteristics, many of which seem to me unattractive, be there for all to see throughout eternity?' Jesus is described in 1 Corinthians as 'the firstfruits of those who have fallen asleep' (15:20). So, as we look at his resurrection body, we get a glimpse of what it may be like for us—the individual essence of each of us 'in beauty glorified', recognisable yet transformed.

Meanwhile, this resurrection hope flows back into our lives, shaping the way we think, speak, and live as we embody God's all-encompassing salvation in the here and now.

For further reflection and action

1. How far are your own beliefs about life after death consistent with each other? How far do they tie up with scripture?

2. How should our understanding of the resurrection body shape our attitude to our present bodies? Can we learn to thank God for the bodies he has given us, as well as praising him for what they will be?

3. How might we seek, in the large and small areas of our lives, to make the world a better place, in preparation for the physical return of Jesus?

48: United we stand, united we end

With all wisdom and understanding, he made known to us the mystery of his will according to his good pleasure, which he purposed in Christ, to be put into effect when the times reach their fulfilment—to bring unity to all things in heaven and on earth under Christ… His purpose was to create in himself one new humanity out of the two, thus making peace, and in one body to reconcile both of them to God through the cross… Make every effort to keep the unity of the Spirit through the bond of peace… until we all reach unity in the faith and in the knowledge of the Son of God and become mature, attaining to the whole measure of the fullness of Christ.

EPHESIANS 1:8–10; 2:15–16; 4:3, 13

In the breathtaking opening of his letter to the Ephesians, Paul outlines the broad sweep of God's plan of salvation, set in place before the foundation of the world. Even as he catalogues the amazing blessings we enjoy in the here and now, he still looks forward to the moment when 'the times reach their fulfilment', when 'all things' will be summed up and gathered together under one head—Christ, the one in whom God will restore harmony to the cosmos.

As the letter goes on, it becomes clear that the ultimate unity of all things—to be fully displayed in Christ—has already had its beginning in the church.

Though dead in sin, enslaved by forces of evil and deserving of wrath, we have been made alive with Christ—only because of God's love and only through faith (2:1–10). But Jesus' death, which brings together God and humanity, also unites people who were formerly alienated from one another. Jews and Gentiles are made into 'one new humanity' (v. 15), reconciled through the cross—both given access to the Father, both citizens of the heavenly temple indwelt by the Spirit, both declaring that defeat of the 'powers' is now certain, and both called to display the wisdom of God (2:11—3:13).

Far from being a passive spectator in this cosmic drama, the church is to live a life worthy of her calling, to display the unity of the Spirit, to grow together in Christ as a unified body, and to reflect to the world God's ultimate plan for the universe, testifying to a comprehensive, all-embracing salvation in lives turned around.

While the vision is cosmic and grand, the outworking is local and specific as we witness to this reconciliation in our everyday existence in particular locations, from Basildon to Bangalore. In doing so, we demonstrate a whole new way of living, before God and with others, that is consistent with our new humanity. And that new way of living starts where we find ourselves every day, with the choices we make every day, with the people we live with every day, with our families and in our jobs, as very ordinary people through whom God is present to the world.

For further reflection and action

1. Paul makes it clear in Ephesians that the church has been included from the outset, not as a supplement to God's plan but as an essential ingredient in his scheme for the universe. How often do we think of our own local church in this way, and what difference might it make to our thinking and practice if we did so?

2. How do we become 'ministers of reconciliation', demonstrating the restoration that the gospel brings to every area of life? Read Ephesians 4—6 and reflect on the way God's design for reconciled lives works out on the ground and in relationship with others.

3. Buy or borrow—and read—a copy of *Practise Resurrection: A Conversation on Growing Up in Christ* by Eugene Peterson (Hodder & Stoughton, 2010), which looks at the theme of 'growing up in Christ' in Ephesians.

49: A world remade

Then I saw 'a new heaven and a new earth,' for the first heaven and the first earth had passed away, and there was no longer any sea. I saw the Holy City, the new Jerusalem, coming down out of heaven from God, prepared as a bride beautifully dressed for her husband. And I heard a loud voice from the throne saying, 'Look! God's dwelling place is now among the people, and he will dwell with them. They will be his people, and God himself will be with them and be their God.'

REVELATION 21:1–3

See, I will create
new heavens and a new earth.
The former things will not be remembered,
nor will they come to mind.
But be glad and rejoice forever
in what I will create,
for I will create Jerusalem to be a delight
and its people a joy.

ISAIAH 65:17–18

Here, then, is the goal of God's redemptive work—a new creation, redeemed and renewed. Not just heaven 'above the bright blue sky', but heaven and earth combined, fused—the two dimensions of reality brought together in a final triumphant rebirth, a new creation that began with Christ's own resurrection. The very physicality of Jesus' resurrection points us to the physicality of the new creation, albeit transformed. Because we believe in his resurrection, we also believe that we too will know 'the resurrection of the body' in the new heaven and the new earth.

It will be an earth purged of evil, put right, glorified as Jesus was glorified at the transfiguration, washed clean of dirt and pollution. There, God 'will wipe every tear from their eyes', and there will be 'no more death or mourning or crying or pain, for the old order of things has passed away' (Revelation

21:4). 'Never again will there be in it an infant who lives but a few days, or an old man who does not live out his years' (Isaiah 65:20).

All that is beautiful and good will survive the purging fire of judgment, leaving a place that we will know and people we will recognise, just as the disciples recognised Jesus, not always straight away but always in a burst of delight.

As sleep that follows fever,
as gold instead of grey,
as freedom after bondage,
as sunrise to the day,
as home to the traveller
and all we long to see,
>   *so is my Lord,*
>   *my living Lord,*
so is my Lord to me.

Bishop Timothy Dudley-Smith wrote these words as a love song to the Lord that we can sing today. But they could equally well describe the way it will be when we are there with him in his new, fresh creation at the end of time, with all of the best of human life fully and comprehensively restored. This is the sure and certain hope that motivates us to bring the love, justice and joy of his kingdom into our world today.

For further reflection and action

1. After a long hard winter, the signs of spring delight the heart—the songs of busy birds, the flowering of early bulbs and the growing warmth of the sun. Rejoice in it all, and

know that the Lord, who filled this damaged and troubled world with such beauty and joy in creation, will recreate a new world both reassuringly familiar and astonishingly different.

2. The Song of Songs is, for many people, a surprising book to find in the Bible. It's a lyrical song in praise of human love—very physical, very sexual, with its love analogies drawn from the natural world, wine and perfume, gold and silver, springtime and blossom, leaping gazelles. Here again the Bible is giving us pointers, in our experience of human love and longing, to the redeemed and perfect creation that God has prepared for those who love him. Read it and praise him.

3. Read Revelation 20—22, noting the 'shadow side' of this amazing hope in those who are excluded from it. What do you believe about the final judgment of God, and why do you believe it?

*

Conclusion

50: To the glory of God

In your relationships with one another, have the same mindset
as Christ Jesus:
    Who, being in very nature God,
    did not consider equality with God something to be used
    to his own advantage;
    rather, he made himself nothing
    by taking the very nature of a servant,
    being made in human likeness.
    And being found in appearance as a man,
    he humbled himself
    by becoming obedient to death—
    even death on a cross!
    Therefore God exalted him to the highest place
    and gave him the name that is above every name,
    that at the name of Jesus every knee should bow,
    in heaven and on earth and under the earth,
    and every tongue acknowledge that Jesus Christ is Lord,
    to the glory of God the Father.
PHILIPPIANS 2:5–11

The Lordship of Christ and the glory of God: there could
hardly be a more appropriate place to end our tour through
scripture.

Actually, it's where we began too, with Jesus as Lord of all
in Colossians 1:15–20. Here, as there, the biblical story of

salvation, never far below the surface of Paul's letters, rises to the top. Here, as there, we are taken from the beginning to the end of all things, an account in which Jesus is central. Here, as there, it is this particular story of this particular person that shapes us, providing a pattern of thinking and living that is ours by dint of being 'in Christ'.

At the centre of the story stands the cross, Paul's words here evoking the horror and shame associated with the public execution of criminals. Yet, that scandalous cross was central to Christ's own determination to press on to Jerusalem, showing the true nature of God's self-giving love. And the cross is central to our understanding of what it means to be a disciple, to follow in his footsteps in serving others: his death not only brings about redemption but also provides a model for our lives.

Even then, the cross is not the end of the story, for God raised Jesus to a place of highest status and assigned him a name that reflects his vindication, with the result that all will confess him 'Lord'. Paul's language deliberately echoes Isaiah 45:22–23, with Christ receiving the glory that God says is reserved for him alone. Beyond this, the confession would have carried political overtones, perhaps especially in Philippi, a colony of the Roman empire in which emperors were proclaimed as 'Lord'. The church's worship of Jesus as Lord not only qualifies the empire's rule but also anticipates the confession that will be offered by the whole universe— the sovereignty of Christ over everything.

This, no doubt, had profound implications for the daily life of Christians in Philippi, and of Christians everywhere since. We 'work out' our salvation, with God himself working in us 'in order to fulfil his good purpose' (Philippians 2:12– 13), concretely applied in our relations with each other and our integrity of witness in the world, where confessing him as Lord means committing to a way of life marked by his Lordship.

And all for the glory of God.

For further reflection and action

1. Some scholars think that this passage in Philippians might be an early hymn, predating the letter itself and thus forming one of the oldest parts of the New Testament. It could have been a poetic celebration and confession of Jesus as Lord sung by groups of Christians, which puts us in touch with very early expressions of faith in Christ. Reflect on the significance of this possibility and turn it into an opportunity for praise.

2. Read Philippians 2:5–11 again, thinking about some of the suggestions for the background of the passage. Which, if any, provides the best fit with the passage, and why?

   - Personified divine Wisdom, who leaves her dwelling-place with God to come into the world to be with humankind (Proverbs 8:22–31).
   - A contrast between Jesus and the first human beings in the garden of Eden (Genesis 3; compare Romans 5:12–21), emphasising the different choice made by Jesus, whose equality with God was not something to be exploited for his own personal advantage.
   - Parallels with the suffering servant of Isaiah 52:13—53:12, who humbled himself (53:4, 8), was obedient (v. 7) and poured himself out to death (v. 12).

3. Even though there are political implications to calling Jesus 'Lord', the early Christians still submitted to Roman authority, understanding that the emperor had lawful authority delegated by God (see, for example, Romans 13:1–7; 1 Peter 2:13–17). If Jesus, not Caesar, was Lord, why did they act in this way? If it is more fitting to describe the early Christians' approach as 'subversive' rather than directly 'counter-political', how appropriate is it to follow their lead in our own context?

Taking next steps

The end of our particular journey through these readings marks the beginning of other journeys. Several possible routes are suggested in what follows, all of which allow the concerns of this book to be explored further.

Engaging with LICC

The London Institute for Contemporary Christianity seeks to equip Christians and churches for whole-life discipleship in the world. If you would like to find out more about LICC—how to receive quarterly mailings or the weekly emails 'Word for the Week' and 'Connecting with Culture'—please visit www.licc.org.uk, call 020 7399 9555, email mail@licc.org.uk, or write to LICC, St Peter's, Vere Street, London, W1G 0DQ.

In addition, the website (www.licc.org.uk) contains many useful resources, including in the following areas:

- Engaging with the Bible: Check out www.licc.org.uk/engaging-with-the-bible for articles, book reviews and other resources on the Bible.
- Tackling the sacred–secular divide: First published in 2010, Mark Greene's booklet *The Great Divide* outlines the problem of the sacred–secular divide and what we can do

about it. For further information, as well as some resources to accompany the booklet, see www.licc.org.uk/the-great-divide.

• Helping churches become whole-life disciple-making communities: For news and resources related to LICC's Imagine project, set up in partnership with local churches around the UK, see www.licc.org.uk/imagine. Resources include the *Imagine* DVD, which seeks to set out a compelling vision for whole-life missional discipleship in the context of the cultural challenges in the church and contemporary society. In addition, see *Imagine Church: Becoming a whole-life disciple-making church* (IVP, 2012), in which Neil Hudson, Imagine Project Director, draws on lessons gleaned from his extensive experience working with churches.

• Equipping Christians for the frontline of work: The paid workplace is the 'frontline' where Christians in work spend over 40 per cent of their waking lives, have more relationships with non-believers than anywhere else, and have more opportunities to influence the primary drivers of society than in any other place. LICC has a long history of resourcing people in the workplace; for helpful material, including video clips, Bible studies and articles, go to www.licc.org/engaging-with-work.

Engaging with BRF

At the heart of BRF's ministry is a desire to equip adults and children for Christian living—helping them to read and understand the Bible, to explore prayer and to grow as disciples of Jesus. BRF is involved in five distinct yet complementary areas.

- BRF (www.brf.org.uk) resources adults for their spiritual journey through Bible reading notes, books, quiet days and teaching days. BRF also provides the infrastructure that supports our other four specialist ministries.
- Foundations21 (www.foundations21.org.uk) provides innovative, flexible ways for individuals and groups to explore their Christian faith and discipleship through a multimedia internet-based resource.
- Messy Church (www.messychurch.org.uk), led by Lucy Moore, enables churches all over the UK and abroad to reach children and adults beyond the fringes of the church.
- Barnabas in Churches (www.barnabasinchurches.org.uk) helps churches to support, resource and develop their children's ministry with the under-11s more effectively .
- Barnabas in Schools (www.barnabasinschools.org.uk) enables primary school children and teachers to explore Christianity creatively and bring the Bible alive within RE and Collective Worship.

To find out more, visit any of the websites listed above. To order BRF books, please go to www.brfonline.org.uk.

Reading the story of life

All of the following titles offer an overview of the 'big story' of scripture and explore, in different ways, its implications for thinking and living as Christians in the contemporary world. They complement the broad outline and approach adopted in this book, and reading one or two of them would help to reinforce your knowledge and understanding of the Bible's grand narrative.

Christopher Ash, *Remaking a Broken World: The Heart of the Bible Story* (Authentic, 2010).

A Bible overview based around the theme of the 'gathering' and 'scattering' of God's people in the biblical storyline, emphasising that 'the local church is at the heart of the Bible story, that it is close to the heart of the purposes of God, and that it is how a broken world will be remade'.

Craig G. Bartholomew and Michael W. Goheen, *The Drama of Scripture: Finding Our Place in the Biblical Story* (SPCK, 2006).

This is one of the best books to explore the biblical 'big story' and its significance in developing a distinctively Christian worldview. The authors trace the theme of the kingdom of God in six acts through scripture.

- Act 1: God establishes his kingdom: creation
- Act 2: Rebellion in the kingdom: fall
- Act 3: The king chooses Israel: redemption initiated
- Interlude: A kingdom story waiting for an ending: the intertestamental period
- Act 4: The coming of the king: redemption accomplished
- Act 5: Spreading the news of the king: the mission of the church
- Act 6: The return of the king: redemption completed

D.A. Carson, *The God Who is There: Finding Your Place in God's Story* (Baker Books, 2010).

This book guides readers through the big story of the Bible, with a special focus on the God who constantly takes the initiative in his relationship with men and women. A separate leader's guide for groups is also available, containing discussion questions and broader theological and pastoral reflections.

Mike Erre, *Why the Bible Matters: Recovering Its Significance in an Age of Suspicion* (Harvest House, 2010).

About half the book goes through the biblical story while the other half explores the significance of finding our place in the story.

Graeme Goldsworthy, *Gospel and Kingdom: A Christian Interpretation of the Old Testament* (Paternoster, 1981), reprinted in *The Goldsworthy Trilogy* (Paternoster, 2000).

Goldsworthy argues for a threefold idea woven throughout scripture, which is 'God's people, in God's place, under God's rule'. When we use that as a rubric, we can see God's kingdom in Eden, with Adam and Eve (God's people) living in the garden (in God's place) under God's rule. But, he says, we see the same motifs again as the biblical story goes on, with the kingdom revealed in Israel's history, the kingdom revealed in prophecy, and the kingdom revealed in Christ.

Philip Greenslade, *A Passion for God's Story: Discovering Your Place in God's Strategic Plan* (Paternoster, 2002).

A helpful book, working through the main contours of the biblical story.

Winn Griffin, *God's EPIC Adventure: Changing Our Culture by the Story We Live and Tell* (Harmon Press, 2007).

A large-format book, with a 'workbook' approach (with learning objectives and questions).

Ian Paul and Philip Jensen, *What's the Bible All About? Understanding the Story of the Bible*, Grove Biblical Series 40 (Grove, 2006).

An excellent booklet-length treatment outlining the biblical story.

Vaughan Roberts, *God's Big Picture: Tracing the Story-line of the Bible* (IVP, 2002, reissued in a larger format in 2009).

Influenced by Goldsworthy (above), this book organises the biblical storyline around the theme of kingdom, which is then traced through scripture in several stages:

1. The pattern of the kingdom
2. The perished kingdom
3. The promised kingdom
4. The partial kingdom
5. The prophesied kingdom
6. The present kingdom
7. The proclaimed kingdom
8. The perfected kingdom

Michael D. Williams, *Far as the Curse is Found: The Covenant Story of Redemption* (P&R, 2005).

This one looks at the scriptural story of redemption from the perspective of God's covenant with his people.

Following the Lord of life

The readings in this book may have provoked an interest in investigating further whole-life discipleship. The following list offers a variety of suggestions, covering the being and making of disciples as well as theological reflection on discipleship and spiritual formation more generally.

Tim Chester, *The Ordinary Hero: Living the Cross and Resurrection* (IVP, 2009).

Explores the implications of the cross and resurrection for the pattern of discipleship.

Charles H. Dunahoo, *Making Kingdom Disciples: A New Framework* (P&R, 2005).

Outlines a holistic, covenantal, kingdom-oriented approach to discipleship, exploring its implications for epistemology (that is, how we know what we know), worldview and our engagement with the world.

Mark Greene and Tracy Cotterell (eds.), *Let My People Grow: Making Disciples Who Make a Difference in Today's World* (Authentic, 2006).

A collection of short, helpful essays by a mixture of academics and church leaders, which grew out of a consultation on disciple-making held at the London Institute for Contemporary Christianity.

Julian Hardyman, *Maximum Life: All for the Glory of God* (IVP, 2009).

First published in 2006 as *Glory Days*, this provides an excellent exploration of the notion that God is as much concerned with our family, hobbies and politics as with our prayer life, Bible reading and church attendance.

Jonathan Lunde, *Following Jesus, the Servant King: A Biblical Theology of Covenantal Discipleship*, Biblical Theology for Life (Zondervan, 2010).

An academic treatment, where the main theological drivers are 'covenant' (its grace and its demands) and 'christology' (Jesus as the Servant King).

Scot McKnight, *One.Life: Jesus Calls, We Follow* (Zondervan, 2010).

A valuable reminder that following Jesus involves the whole of a disciple's life.

Eugene Peterson, *Christ Plays in Ten Thousand Places: A Conversation in Spiritual Theology* (Hodder & Stoughton, 2005).

The first volume in Peterson's 'Spiritual Theology' series. Check out the others too.

Bob Roberts, Jr., *Real-Time Connections: Linking Your Job to God's Global Work* (Zondervan, 2010).

An important reminder that the great commission is not just for church workers but for everyday, ordinary Christians in their normal walks of life.

John Stott, *The Radical Disciple: Wholehearted Christian Living* (IVP, 2010).

A warm-hearted exploration of eight neglected aspects of discipleship.

John Valentine, *Follow Me: Becoming a Liberated Disciple* (IVP, 2009).

Helpfully structured around a progression from the personal to the corporate to the cosmic, from an individual's following of Jesus to the renewed human race present in the church to God's ultimate plan to renew all creation.

Chick Yuill, *Moving in the Right Circles: Embrace the Discipleship Adventure* (IVP, 2011).

Looks at discipleship as a series of four concentric circles: walking in the company of Jesus, growing in the community of believers, engaging with the culture of the times, and looking to the coming of the King.

*

Notes

1   See Eugene H. Peterson, *Eat This Book: The Art of Spiritual Reading* (Hodder & Stoughton, 2006).

2   A considerable number of others have mapped out the biblical story in similar terms: see, for example, Craig G. Bartholomew and Michael W. Goheen, *The Drama of Scripture: Finding Our Place in the Biblical Story* (SPCK, 2006) and other books mentioned in the 'Taking next steps' section.

3   See Bartholomew and Goheen, *Drama of Scripture*, pp. 1–6.

4   John Stott, *The Contemporary Christian* (IVP, 1992), p. 390.

5   John Milton, *Paradise Lost*, introduced by Philip Pullman (Oxford University Press, 2005), p. 17.

6   Martin Kahler, *The So-Called Historical Jesus and the Historic, Biblical Christ*, trans. Carl E. Braaten (Fortress, 1964), p. 80, n. 121.

7   Tom Wright, *Surprised by Hope* (SPCK, 2007), pp. 78–79.

8   Wright, *Surprised by Hope*, p. 57.

9   Gordon D. Fee, *The First Epistle to the Corinthians* (Eerdmans, 1987), p. 605.

10 Wright, *Surprised by Hope*, p. 166.

11 Wright, *Surprised by Hope*, p. 168.